Moodle 1.9 for Teaching 7-14 Year Olds
Beginner's Guide

Effective e-learning for younger students, using Moodle as your Classroom Assistant

Mary Cooch

PACKT PUBLISHING

BIRMINGHAM - MUMBAI

Moodle 1.9 for Teaching 7-14 Year Olds

Beginner's Guide

First published: March 2009

Production Reference: 1200309

Published by Packt Publishing Ltd.
32 Lincoln Road
Olton
Birmingham, B27 6PA, UK.

ISBN 978-1-847197-14-6

www.packtpub.com

Cover Image by Parag Kadam (Paragvkadam@gmail.com)

Credits

Author

Mary Cooch

Reviewers

Andy Baker

Clive Wright

Garvin Hicking

Acquisition Editor

David Barnes

Development Editor

Nikhil Bangera

Technical Editor

Mehul Shetty

Copy Editor

Sumathi Sridhar

Indexer

Monica Ajmera

Production Editorial Manager

Abhijeet Deobhakta

Editorial Team Leader

Akshara Aware

Project Team Leader

Lata Basantani

Project Coordinator

Rajashree Hamine

Proofreader

Dirk Manuel

Production Coordinator

Dolly Dasilva

Aparna Bhagat

Cover Work

Dolly Dasilva

About the author

Mary Cooch has taught Languages and Geography in the UK for over 20 years. She manages several websites, even more Moodles, and runs her own Moodle blog. A Moodle Certified Teacher, she now spends part of her working week travelling the country as a VLE trainer specializing in Moodle. She regularly promotes its benefits in schools and has a deep understanding of what works best for younger students. Known online as the *moodlefairy*, Mary is a frequent contributor to the help forums of www.moodle.org where she aims to enthuse others with her passion for this Open Source Virtual Learning Environment.

Mary works at Our Lady's Catholic High School, in Preston, Lancashire, UK.

I would like to express my thanks, at Packt Publishing, to David, Rajashree, Nikhil, and Mehul for their support and encouragement; at home, to my family for allowing me the time and space to write; and at school, to Mark, for being Mark.

About the reviewers

Andy Baker is Head of ICT at Bishop Challoner Catholic College in Birmingham. He has a strong interest for innovation, particularly in education, and feels that technology, if used effectively, is fundamental in motivating learners to learn.

Prior to becoming a teacher, Andy worked as a Software Engineer within the Telecoms sector. From his experience in working on multi-million pound projects in the industry, to using technology for teaching and learning, Andy is keen to show that you don't necessarily need to have an excessive budget (which is usually the case for most schools) to make valuable use of future, and indeed traditional, technologies. Heavily-involved in the deployment and installation of Moodle Course Management Systems, Andy spends a lot of his time training teaching staff within the education sector.

When he's not teaching, or Moodling, Andy likes to spend quality time with his wife Vicci, and their daughters Francesca and Grace.

Andy lives in Worcestershire, England and can be reached at abaker@iteach.uk.com.

Clive Wright has been a senior teacher in charge of E-learning, as well as a secondary school advisor working with educational establishments, and leading on, amongst other things, the use of Information and Communication Technology in the classroom. He has extensive experience in leading teacher training on the use of new technologies in education. Clive believes that technology can engage and excite young people in their education, enhancing their learning as well as making the learning experience more enjoyable and thereby more effective. He is the director of a website software company—www.nomumbojumbo.com— and he also works with schools, setting up Moodle environments and providing Moodle training. Clive lives in the medieval cathedral city of Lichfield in England with his wife Rebecca and four children: Ellie, Beth, Hannah and Will. He can be contacted on cwright@iteach.uk.com.

Garvin Hicking is a passionate Web developer, engaged in Open Source projects such as Serendipity (Lead Developer) or phpMyAdmin. He works at the internet agency Faktor E GmbH in Bonn (Germany). To date, he has been involved in writing or reviewing several books about PHP, the most recent one being the official documentation of the PHP-Blog application Serendipity. Aside from his professional work, he and his girlfriend enjoy taking professional photographs.

Table of Contents

Preface

This is not a book for geeks. This book will not tell you about PHP, HTML, or anything else that you don't need to know. This is a practical book for teachers written by a teacher with two decades of experience, latterly, in using Moodle to motivate youngers. The aim of this book is to give you some hints and advice on how to get your Moodle course up and running with useful content that your students will actually want to go and learn from on a regular basis.

We will assume that you have an installation of Moodle that is managed by somebody else, so that you are only responsible for creating and delivering course content. Throughout the book, we will be building a course from scratch, adaptable for ages 7-14, on Rivers and Flooding. It could be any topic however, as Moodle lends itself to all subjects and people of all ages.

What this book covers

Chapter 1 teaches us how to capture the attention of our young students and entice them into the Moodle course. It starts with a blank course page, and looks at how to brighten this up with useful side blocks, colorful fonts and attractive images.

Chapter 2 teaches us how to upload to our course page lessons, homework, and worksheets that we have already made in programs such as Microsoft Word or PowerPoint. We will also learn how to create lessons directly in Moodle by using web pages.

Chapter 3 gets the students to interact with us, the teachers, and with each other in Moodle. This chapter combines classroom tasks with Moodle activities in a role-play project, which will get the students thinking and collaborating. It gets them discussing issues in forums and secure chat rooms. It gets the students sharing resources in wikis, glossaries, and databases and find out how to have them send work to us (the teachers) which we can mark online with Moodle recording the grades automatically for us.

Chapter 4 gives us ideas for introducing, practicing, and consolidating learning through the use of online activities such as quizzes, matching exercises, and crosswords made with a program called Hot Potatoes. We learn how, at the click of a button, we can have differentiated exercises for students of varying abilities—and then go have a break while Moodle does all of the marking!

Chapter 5 teaches us how to enhance learning with some easy-to-set-up games, one of which Moodle can mark for us. So while the students are playing and enjoying, the grade book is keeping the scores updated.

Chapter 6 is concerned with sound and vision. Here we get the students involved in producing multimedia content for Moodle—and get creative ourselves too!

Chapter 7 is all about the Wonderful World of Web 2.0. This chapter harnesses what the young students are familiar with by looking at some free online applications that can be used in Moodle both by us and by our students.

Chapter 8 deals with the 'nitty gritty' of uploading and displaying resources in Moodle. It explains how to ensure that everything works properly, not just for teachers but also for students. We learn how to make resources accessible to children who don't have Microsoft Office. We also discover alternative methods of displaying worksheets and slideshows, and investigate ways of resizing images to use on our course page.

Chapter 9 gives a taste of Moodle Level 2! It looks at how we can use the more advanced features of Moodle, plus some optional extras, to enhance our teaching further. We learn how to use the Lesson module, and how to use RSS feeds. We consider some non-standard modules, such as the Questionnaire and Certificate modules, and end our journey by making our Moodle course page look more like a regular web page.

What you need for this book

No specific technologies are needed, although it is assumed the reader will play the role of a teacher in the Moodle course that is set up for them. It is desirable, though not essential, to have access to Microsoft Word and PowerPoint.

Who is this book for

This book is for regular, non-technical, teachers of pre-teen or early teens. It assumes no prior knowledge of Moodle and no particular expertise of anything on the Web. Classroom assistants may also find this book a very useful resource.

Conventions

In this book, you will find a number of styles of text that distinguish between different kinds of information. Here are some examples of these styles, and an explanation of their meaning.

Code words in text are shown as follows: "But that's not all! When we edited the `.xml` file (called `words`), it automatically linked itself to the other games in the folder, too."

New terms and **important words** are shown in bold. Words that you see on the screen, in menus or dialog boxes for example, appear in our text like this: "Choose the option **Link to a file or website** ".

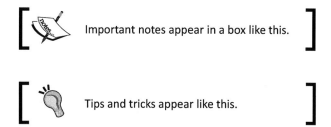

Important notes appear in a box like this.

Tips and tricks appear like this.

Reader feedback

Feedback from our readers is always welcome. Let us know what you think about this book—what you liked or may have disliked. Reader feedback is important for us to develop titles that you really get the most out of.

To send us general feedback, simply drop an email to feedback@packtpub.com, and mention the book title in the subject of your message.

If there is a book that you need and would like to see us publish, please send us a note via the **SUGGEST A TITLE** form on www.packtpub.com, or send an email to suggest@packtpub.com.

If there is a topic that you have expertise in and you are interested in either writing or contributing to a book on, see our author guide on www.packtpub.com/authors.

Customer support

Now that you are the proud owner of a Packt book, we have a number of things to help you to get the most from your purchase.

Errata

Although we have taken every care to ensure the accuracy of our contents, mistakes do happen. If you find a mistake in one of our books—maybe a mistake in text or code—we would be grateful if you would report this to us. By doing so, you can save other readers from frustration, and help us to improve subsequent versions of this book. If you find any errata, please report them by visiting http://www.packtpub.com/support, selecting your book, clicking on the **let us know** link, and entering the details of your errata. Once your errata are verified, your submission will be accepted and the errata added to any list of existing errata. Any existing errata can be viewed by selecting your title from http://www.packtpub.com/support.

Piracy

Piracy of copyright material on the Internet is an ongoing problem across all media. At Packt, we take the protection of our copyright and licenses very seriously. If you come across any illegal copies of our works in any form on the Internet, please provide us with the location address or website name immediately, so that we can pursue a remedy.

Please contact us at copyright@packtpub.com with a link to the suspected pirated material.

We appreciate your help in protecting our authors, and our ability to bring you valuable content.

Questions

You can contact us at questions@packtpub.com if you are having a problem with any aspect of this book, and we will do our best to address it.

1
Getting started

We're at the very start of our journey here. We know where we are heading—we want to create a fun-filled, interesting, interactive, and informative learning environment for our young students. We want them to have access to all of our resources that would normally be on paper, plus any new activities that we hope are out there, but that we haven't actually discovered! Ideally, we'd like a situation where our initial efforts will be rewarded by saving us a lot of time in the long term. We want Moodle to occupy our students usefully, mark their work, and record their scores so that we don't have to do it. A tall order, but one that is perfectly possible!

In this chapter, we shall:

- Take a tour of the Moodle course page to get familiar with all of the options that we have; so that we are ready to set it up for our classes
- Choose the most suitable layout for our course, and make each section attractive to the students
- Take a look, add, and edit the blocks on either side of our work area to make these blocks useful for us and our class
- Find out where to store our work when we start putting it on Moodle
- Add text and images to our work area to improve its appearance
- Learn how to make **click here** links to various web sites for our students to easily access them

First impressions

Let's assume you've been given an empty Moodle course page. When you first go to your course page, you'll probably see something that looks like this:

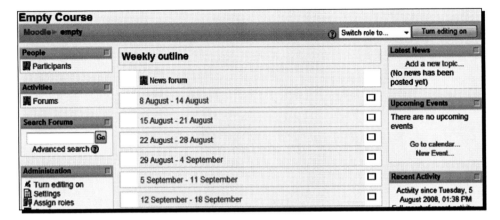

Don't be disheartened if this doesn't mean much to you at this stage. If you were to flick through to the end of the book, you would find our completed work far more welcoming:

There are three columns; two narrow ones on the right and left, containing some blocks, and a wider column in the middle. This wider column is the work area, to which we will start adding our teaching materials (this will be covered in detail in Chapter 2). The name of the course (**Empty Course**, for now) appears on the upper left, and an abbreviated version (**empty**) will appear in the bar below it (the bar is called a **breadcrumb trail**). The block called **Administration** is just for the teachers. It allows us (teachers) to perform various actions for our course. Let's start by changing the course name to what we want, and setting up the work area to something more suitable for us.

Don't be put off by the word **Course**. A course can be anything you want it to be—a teacher's class page, a single unit of work (such as ours), a project, a year's lessons shared among a group of teachers, and so on.

Time for action-customising our course page

1. In the **Administration** block, click on **Settings**.

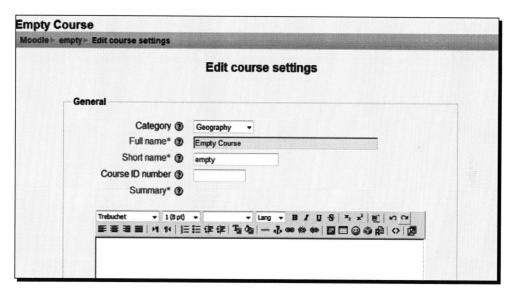

2. Next to **Full name**, type in the full name of your course (such as **Rivers and Flooding**).

3. Next to **Short name**, give your course an abbreviation, which will be seen in the navigation bar. For our example course, we'll use **R & F**.

4. In **Summary**, write a sentence or two to explain what the course is about.

5. Scroll down to the sections shown in the following screenshot:

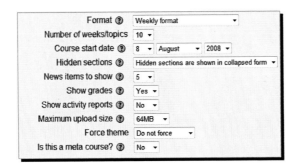

6. For Format, you can use the default value of Date format to include one section per date in your course page, or you can select Weekly format to include one section per week, or select Topic format to use numbered sections that you can set up as you like. For this example, we will select Topic format.

7. In the **Number of weeks/topics** field, choose the number of days, weeks, or topics that you want to include on your course page (you can change this at any time). For this example, we will specify 4.

8. If you want your course to start on a particular date (and not immediately), specify this date in the **Course start date** field.

9. For now, as a beginner, this much will be enough.

 If at first you don't know what it means, it's safe to ignore it!

10. Click on **Save** and return to course. Your course page should now look something like this:

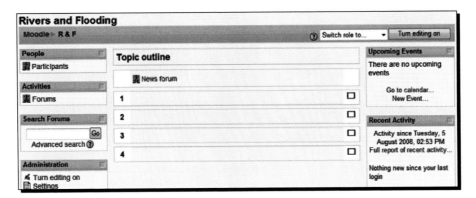

What just happened?

We just began customizing our course page to how we want it to look. We've now got the title we want, and the middle section (where our work will go) is now divided into separate numbered sections—four, for us—which will help us to organize our project. At the moment, there's nothing next to these numbers. We need to get into each section, give it a heading, and prepare it so that we can add our worksheets and lessons, which we will do in future chapters of this book. There's something called a **News forum** too, which I'll describe later. We've also still got those blocks on either side. Obviously, the Administration block is essential, but what about the others? What are they for? Do we need them? And how do we change them? In fact, how do we change anything on the page?

Making changes on the course page

If you point your cursor at one of the sections in the middle and start typing—nothing happens! We can't actually add any text or make any alterations until we have clicked on the **Turn editing on** button which is on the upper right of the screen. (You can also get to it by clicking on the Administration block) When you do, everything looks different, as shown in the next screenshot. Don't panic!

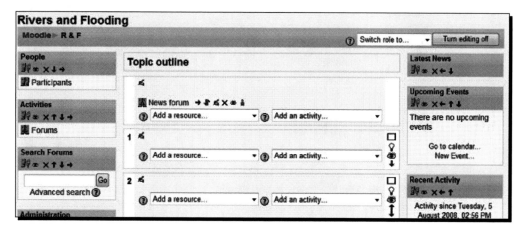

A lot of symbols (icons) have appeared. These symbols have different roles in helping us to edit the course. They help us to add content, delete content, or alter what's already there. Let's take a tour of the blocks, and use this as a way to understand these icons.

Getting the best out of the side blocks

Every course in Moodle has a central work area and a selection of blocks on either side. These blocks serve various purposes such as: telling you the latest news, letting you know who's online, displaying quiz results, and so on. Shortly, we'll have a look at the blocks available, and I'll give you my thoughts on how useful they might be. Some schools may decide for you which blocks you must have, and the blocks that should be made **sticky** throughout Moodle. If you're allowed to have your own blocks, then the next section will show you how you can move them around and take away the ones that you don't really need. First, let's take a closer look at the **Activities** block. The following screenshot shows the **Activities** block, although the icons shown are available in every block.

Time for action-moving, adding, and deleting blocks

Let's learn how to add and delete blocks into our Moodle course page.

1. **To hide a block** from students, click on the eye. (You will still be able to see it greyed out.) Click again to make it visible to students.

2. **To delete a block** from the course page, click on the **X.** (You can add it again later; it's not gone forever.)

3. **To move a block up,** click on the up arrow (blocks are moved up one block at a time).

4. **To move a block down,** click on the down arrow (blocks are moved down one block at a time).

5. **To move a block to the other side,** click the left or right arrow (the block will go across be positioned at the other side and to the bottom of the column).

6. **To add a new block,** find the block called **Blocks,** and then click on **Add** (as shown in the following screenshot).

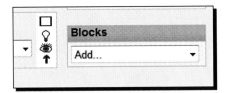

7. The **face icons** are to do with who can see and edit the blocks (ignore these for now).

Useful (and less useful) blocks

Here's a table of the standard blocks that are available in Moodle, and that you could have on your course page (if you're allowed). I've explained what they do, and what I think about them:

Block name	What it does	Why use it
Activities	Shows the different activities that you've set up	If you want your students to get to certain activities quickly, or see them listed
Administration	The teacher's admin block	Essential for you, and it's where your students can see their grades
Blog menu/tags	Allows you to add and view blog entries and keywords in blogs	Not really necessary as a block (we look at blogs in chapter 6)
Calendar	A calendar where you can show course, individual, or site wide events	Useful if you have a lot of events that you want to remind your students about
Courses	Lists students courses	A quick way for them to get around their courses
Course description	Shows the course **summary** that you put in the course settings	Not really essential—they're doing the course now, after all!
Global search	Lets you search all of Moodle	Has to be switched on by your admin—and you don't need it—leave it out!
HTML	A blank block for your own use	Very handy—more details later
Latest news	Displays what's in the news forum	If you want that, it's fine!
Loan calculator	It Calculates interest on loans	Someone, somewhere must need it—but not us
Mentees block	Advanced block allowing mentors to 'watch' students	We don't need it at this stage
Messages	Moodle's instant messaging service	Needs to be switched on by your admin; useful for instant communication, but younger students may find it very distracting!
Online users	Shows who's accessing your course online at the moment	Useful for making sure that everyone's there, on task

Block name	What it does	Why use it
People	Lists those enrolled in your course, and when they last visited your course page	Another useful block to keep a check on your participants.
Quiz results	Displays recent quiz results	Handy for encouraging competition amongst students, by providing a league table of scores.
Recent activity	Who's done what and when	Useful for students to see what's new, and for teachers to see who's sent in their work
Random glossary entry	Shows a glossary entry at a certain time (if you've got a glossary)	Think about this when we are making a glossary in chapter 3; up to you
Remote RSS feeds	Shows news feeds of your choice	Can be very useful— we'll look at this in the final chapter
Search forums	Allows students to search through forum entries	Don't bother with this; I've never found it useful for my classes
Section links	A quick way to get to a numbered section	If you want to, fine and good; useful if your sections are very long and need a lot of scrolling down
Upcoming events	Information about what's coming soon, taken from the calendar or activity deadlines	If you have a lot of events or deadlines it's useful.

Have a go hero-get the right choice of blocks for your course!

Ok, now it's time to put the theory into practice! For our purposes, the best blocks will probably be the ones listed below. Using the instructions on the previous pages, delete the ones we don't want, add the new ones, and then arrange them equally on either side of the middle section! Let's have:

- A **People** block
- An **Administration** block (of course!)
- A **Courses** block
- A **Calendar** block
- A **Messages** block
- An **HTML** block (which we'll customize now)

Making our own side blocks in Moodle

When you've added a new block and chosen **HTML**, you'll see that you get an extra icon at the top that the other blocks don't have. This icon varies according to the version and style (theme) of Moodle that you have, but usually it is something like a pen and paper, or a hand and a pen. This is the **editing icon**. Wherever you see it in Moodle, it takes you to a place where you can add text, images, links, and other more complex stuff to sites. Let's go there!

Time for action-configuring an HTML block

Let's learn how to configure an HTML block for our course page.

1. Click on the editing icon in your HTML block
2. In the **Block Title field**, enter something for use as the title of your block
3. In the **Content field**, type a few words of welcome

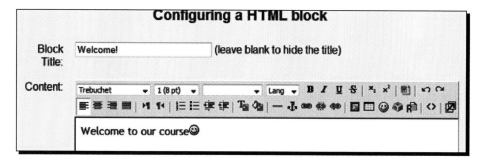

4. Click on **Save** and return to course.

What just happened?

We made a side block of our own! At the moment, it only has a couple of words in it (and a smiley in my case). Later in this chapter, you'll add an image and we'll make it the 'Welcome' block for our new course. I like to use HTML blocks with images to brighten up the page—younger students appreciate this. You can even set them up so that you can click on the image to get to a particular web site, which is both attractive and useful.

As we did this, we came across the editing box—known as the **HTML editor** for the first time, into which we can type text and add images. We're going to investigate it further now as we venture into the middle section—the main focus of our students' learning.

HTML is just a term meaning, web site code, an **HTML block** is one where we can add text that Moodle interprets as code, and displays as we wish. Likewise, in the **HTML editor** we can type the words as we want them to appear, and Moodle will code them (with HTML) to make that happen. We don't need to understand HTML in order to get Moodle to work for us.

Customizing the middle section

It is finally time to get to grips with the middle section—the one we shall be focusing on in the next few chapters. So far, our Rivers and Flooding course has got four empty topic sections. Our next task is to get them ready for action—ready for the materials that we will create and upload, from Chapters 2 onwards.

If you look at the following screenshot, you will see that at the top it says **Topic Outline**. We cannot easily change these words, but we can use the blank space at the top to provide a short description of what our course is about, and we can add headings to each of the four sections.

Remember that to do anything on this page now, we need to have editing turned on (via the button on the upper right) and then, in order to type directly into Moodle, we have to click on the pen or hand or paper icon that we had came across in the HTML block. You can see one above the news forum, and one next to the numbered sections:

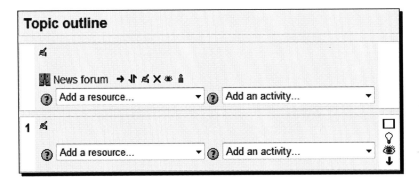

Clicking on the very top one, above the **News forum**, sends us to a page—**Summary of Topic 0**. It would be the same if we had clicked on any of the numbered topics (or weeks, if you've chosen them). It would say **Summary of week/topic** and provide a text box in the **HTML editor**.

Using the HTML editor

We enter our descriptions/headings directly into this box. You will recognize some of the icons from many popular word processing programs, and if you move your cursor over a particular icon, it will give you a hint as to what it does. Younger children like bright colors in a large font, so I'm going to make my headings 'Big' and 'Red':

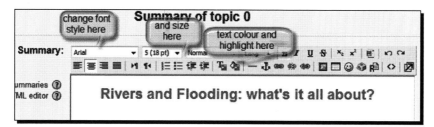

Go along the two layers of icons and find out what they do. Type in some text and experiment! Some are pretty self-explanatory. The following table explains a few of the icons you might find useful, but that are less obvious. The numbers in the table refer to the icons in the following screenshot:

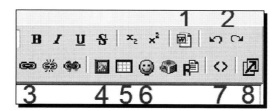

Icon	What it does
1	Improves the look of your text if you paste it in directly from Micrsoft Word
2	Lets you cancel what you just did and revert to an earlier stage
3	Lets you create a link to a web site outside of Moodle
4	Lets you insert an image into the text area
5	Lets you create a table, to improve the layout of your text area
6	Allows you to add smileys
7	Lets you go into the HTML code area (some uses for us later!)
8	Enlarges the text box to make it easier to see and type

Once you've typed in your text and adapted it according to your requirements, scroll down and click **Save changes**. Only then will your efforts be visible on the main course page. Until that moment, you can change whatever you wish.

Have a go hero-give titles to each section of your course

We have just given a heading to **Topic 0**—the top section of our course. If you click on the editing icon for each of the other four topics, you can do exactly the same with them. Remember to change the colour, font style, and size (if you wish) from the rather uninteresting default style. Either go for it and add your own titles to the sections of your course, or practise with the ones we're going to use in our ongoing example. They are:

♦ Famous Rivers of the World

♦ How does a river flow?

♦ Why do rivers flood?

♦ Flooding case studies

What just happened?

We now have headings for each of our topic sections. The page looks more personal and brighter already! A few photographs would enhance it though; we'll put some on the page in a moment.

Soon, it will be time for us to add our teaching materials and activities for students. Perhaps, it might be a sensible time now to find out exactly where all of our materials (including photos) will be stored.

Where does Moodle store our stuff?

Each course in Moodle has its own separate area for storing files such as your worksheets and photographs that you might want to display on the page. Teachers can get to this area (**course files**) by clicking on **Files** in the **Administration** block (students can only see their grades, by the way, and nothing else).

Because we've got nothing in our course yet, this is what we see:

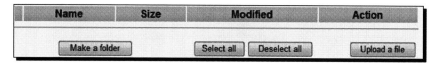

It's a good idea to be organized in your Moodle course, just as you should be with files on your computer, or even paperwork at your home or office. Of course, you could just throw everything at random into this course file storage area, the same way as you'd fling a bill into a drawer in your house. But six months down the line, when every class in your school is using your Moodle daily because you've done it so well, you might regret not having set it up neatly in the first instance! So let's take a moment to do just that.

Time for action-setting up the course files area

Let's learn how to set up a course file area where we can neatly arrange all the files needed for the course.

1. In the **Administration** block, click on **Files**.
2. Click on **Make a folder**.
3. In the box that follows (as shown in the following screenshot), type in **images**.

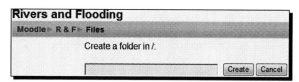

4. You'll be taken to the course files area, where you will see your folder called **images**.

5. Click on your course's short name to return to the main page.

What just happened?

We made a folder in the course files storage area, which is now ready to receive any image that we want to display on our Moodle page. We have to do this because we can neither just directly copy and paste them onto our course pages, nor upload them directly onto the course page. We have to **upload** them first to the storage area, and then decide where and how to display them on the page. (It's important to understand this because it means that you can always keep some worksheets in storage before actually displaying them on your page, if you want). In Chapter 2, we'll make another folder for our worksheets. From now on, when we need to transfer items from our own computer (or USB drive), we'll put them straight into an appropriately-named folder to make it easier for us (or any other teacher sharing our course) to locate them later.

Folders can have any name of your choice. You can name them after the topics; you can divide them up into Word-processed documents and slideshows, or each teacher can have his or her own individual folder. It doesn't matter, as long as you have a system!

Brightening up the course page with images

"What is the use of a book", said Alice, "without pictures?"

I'm sometimes fortunate enough to be given temporary access to other schools' Moodle sites. Almost invariably, the web sites that are most successful in attracting the young students are the ones that catch the eye immediately on entering the course. Those with nothing more than the default text and a long list of exercises (usually named worksheet 1, worksheet 2, and so on) are barren and lonely places, devoid of any youthful spirit. I can't emphasize this enough—we as adults might think it's the content that matters (and of course, that's true), but our children will be drawn into our Moodle course by a colourful photo or a smiley icon. Once they're there, we can help them learn!

We don't have to be qualified web designers to make our course page more attractive. We've made a start already, with our headings. Lets' now add a small, relevant photo to each topic section. By small I mean, a photo with a size of not more than 200 x 200 pixels. (We'll look at photo resizing in Chapter 7.) Although you can upload a large photo and resize it by dragging at its edges, this distorts the image in Moodle, and doesn't display as well as it ought to.

You can't really copy and paste images from Google onto your course page. Apart from copyright issues, this doesn't always work. You might be able to get away with this in PowerPoint, but in Moodle, it's more reliable if you save your chosen image to your hard drive first, and then upload it to the file storage area we've just seen.

Time for action-uploading images to our Moodle page

Now that we have set up our Moodle course page. Let's make it a little more attractive by adding images.

1. Turn on editing.

2. Click on the editing icon for a topic section (for us, **Topic 1**).

3. Click on the icon that helps you insert an image , as shown in the following screenshot:

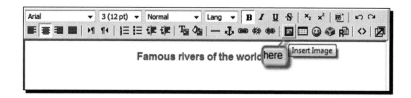

4. In the box that is displayed next, click on the folder named **images**.

5. In the box that is displayed next, scroll down to where you can see the **Browse** button.

6. Click on the **Browse** button and locate the image that you want, on your computer. (It should either have the extension `.jpg` or `.gif`.)

7. Select your image and then click **Open**, and it will appear in the **Browse** box above.

8. Click on the **Upload** button.

9. Your image's filename will appear in the leftmost section of the next screen. Click on it, and it will be previewed in the rightmost section:

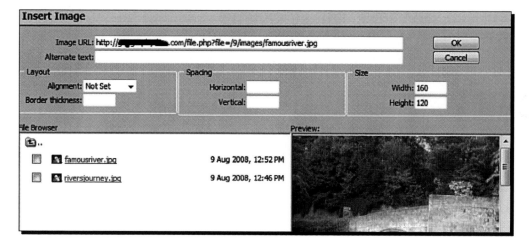

10. Note that your image's filename is also displayed at the top where it says **Image URL**.

11. Underneath that, add some descriptive text, explaining the photo, in the **Alternate text** box. (Don't just say **photo**!)

12. Click on **OK**.

13. Click on **Save changes**, to make the image appear on your course page.

What just happened?

We've now added our first image to our Moodle course page to brighten it up! It probably seems like an extremely long-winded way of adding an image, but that's only because it's the first time that we did it. Additionally, remember that we made a folder to put all of our images in, and we won't need to do that again. The more often that you upload images, the quicker it becomes. I can add images now in a matter of seconds; you will be able to do so as well, with practice. Just bear in mind the following points:

- Get your image to the right size before you upload it to Moodle.

- Make sure that you are uploading an image file—usually having the extension, `.jpg` or `.gif` (more on this, later).

- Don't copy and paste an image from the internet. If the site—that the image comes from—ever goes offline, your image will vanish, and you'll end up with a red X.

Have a go hero-add an image to your HTML block

Remember our **Welcome** block? If you click on the editing icon there, Moodle will operate in exactly the same way as it does with the topic summaries. Go back and insert an image there! (Again, not too large an image!) And then move the block so that it is positioned on the upper left of our page, where the eye will naturally start reading from, when a student enters the course. You should now have something like this:

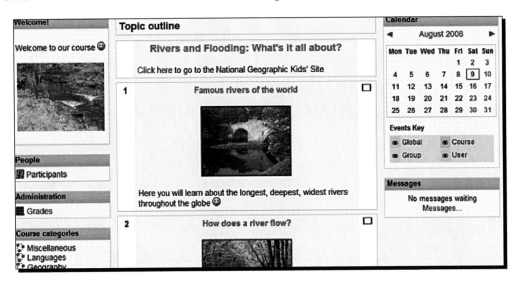

Compare this screenshot with our first view of the course page, as shown here:

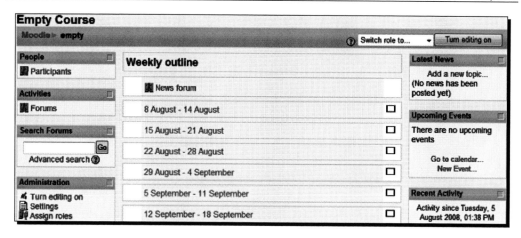

Better already!

> If you want to get rid of the **News forum**, as I have, then you need to change the number of news items to 0 in the course settings, in the **Administration** block. Then, with the editing turned on, click on the **X** icon next to the **News forum**, to delete it.

Adding links to other web sites in Moodle

Did you notice that I made a **click here** in Topic 0 that links to the National Geographic Kids' site? This is a really useful feature of Moodle, as it saves you from having to write a web site on the board or in a worksheet, and it saves your students having to copy it – and then retype it when they get it wrong. One click, and they're there! Let's end our introductory tour of our Moodle course by adding a relevant web site link (or hyperlink)

Time for action-making a 'click here' link to a web site

There are two ways in which we can link to other web sites in Moodle. For now, we're going to use the HTML editor and make a link in one of our topic summaries.

1. Turn on editing, and then click on the editing icon in one of the topic summaries

2. Type in some text.

3. Select the text that you want the students to click on to go to your chosen web site (It doesn't have to say **click here**—it can say anything you want).

4. Click on the **chain** icon, as shown in the following screenshot.

5. In the box that is displayed next, type in (or copy and paste) the URL of the web site that you want them to visit, next to **URL**. (If you copy and paste, make sure that you only have one **http://** at the start.)

6. Next to **Title**, enter the name of the site, which will be seen when students hover their cursor over the link.

7. Make sure that **Target** specifies **New window**.

8. Click on **OK.**

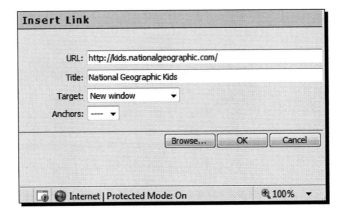

9. Back in the HTML editor, scroll down and click on **Save Changes** (don't worry about **anchors**- these are used to send you to various parts of your course, but at this stage we don't really need them).

What just happened?

Selecting some text (for example, **click here**) and clicking on the **chain** icon enabled us to link directly to a useful site for our students. Choosing **New Window** means that the site will open in a pop-up window. The children can close it with the **X** and will still have Moodle open on their screen. If you test it out yourselves, you'll see what I mean. The linked site can be resized and moved around, without losing Moodle.

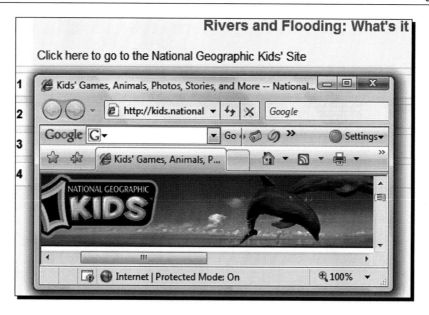

Another neat feature for us to take advantage of!

Summary

In this chapter, we got to know our new Moodle course page and started customizing it with ready-to-add materials and student activities. We performed the following tasks:

- Altered the layout to suit our subject, students, and teaching style
- Looked at how to move and add useful blocks on either sides of the main work area
- Organized our file storage bank into appropriately- named folders
- Learned how to add text and images to our course page to make it more attractive to young children
- Learned how to add clickable links to external web sites from our course

There is nothing magical about what we have achieved so far—it's all very basic. Just think which web site would your young students would be more inclined to visit and linger on—a bare page with a list of numbered topics waiting for an even longer list of Word-processed documents, or a bright, colorful web site that is full of potential, waiting for the fun, resources, and activities that we will produce in the following chapters? Style over content? We've got the style—now let's get some content!

2
Adding worksheets and resources

This chapter is all about saving energy. Not only our own, but the world's too! Moodle's main attraction, to many teachers, is the fact that you can upload all of those worksheets that you hand out in class (and that your students lose). When you've done it once, they are there for as long as you need them—so you don't have to find and print them off the next time you do that topic, and fewer trees will be felled in the name of education! We're teaching the topic of Rivers and Flooding; so to start with, we'll need to introduce our class to some basic facts about rivers and how they work. We aren't going to generate any new stuff yet; we're just going to upload to Moodle what we have already produced in previous years.

In this chapter, we shall:

- Put an information sheet about the River Thames into Moodle
- Load a whole week's slideshows about River processes into Moodle in a neat folder
- Make a **click here** type link (this is known as a **hyperlink**) to the River Thames web site
- Create a worksheet about flooding by typing it straight into Moodle
- Make our page a bit prettier now that we've got some real stuff on it

Putting a worksheet on Moodle

The way Moodle works is that we must first upload our worksheet into the course file storage area (as we did in Chapter 1 with our **images** folder). Then, in that central section of our course page, we make a link to the worksheet from some appropriately chosen words. Our students click on these words to get to the worksheet. We've got an introductory factsheet (done in Word) about the River Thames. Let's get it into Moodle:

Time for action-uploading a factsheet on to Moodle

We need to get the worksheet uploaded into Moodle. To get this done, we have to follow a few simple steps.

1. Go to your course page and click on the **Turn editing on** button, as shown in the following screenshot:

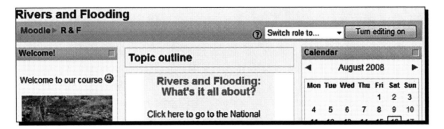

2. Don't worry about all of the new symbols (icons) that appear. In the section you want the worksheet to be displayed, so look for these two boxes:

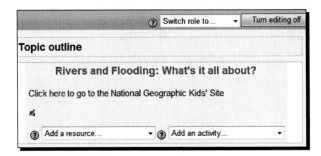

3. Click on the **Add a resource** box (I'll go through all its options when we have a recap, later).

4. Select a link to a file or web site.

5. In **Name**, type the text that you want the students to click on, and in **Summary** (if you want) add a short description. The following screenshot gives an example of this:

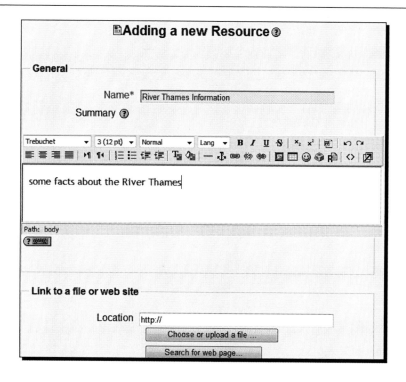

6. Once you're done with the above steps, click on **Choose or upload a file**. This takes you to the course files storage area (we have seen this in Chapter 1).

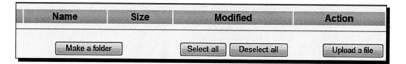

7. Click on **Make a folder**, and in the dialog box that is displayed, choose a suitable name for the folder all your worksheets will be stored in (we'll use **Worksheets**).

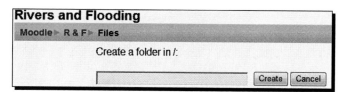

8. Click on **Create**.

9. Click on the folder that you just created (It will be empty except for `Parent Folder`, which takes you back to the main course files).

10. Click on **Upload a file**. You'll be prompted to browse your computer's hard drive for the worksheet.

11. Find the worksheet, select it with your cursor and click **Open**. It will appear as shown in the following screenshot:

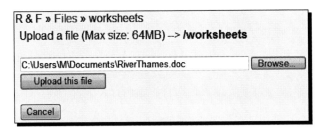

12. Click **Upload this file**. Once the file has been uploaded, it will appear as shown in the following screenshot:

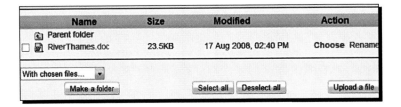

What just happened?

We just uploaded our first ever worksheet to Moodle. It's now in the course files. Next, we need to make a link on the page that students can click on to get to that worksheet.

I know what you're thinking! Thirteen steps, and there's still no sign of our River Thames worksheet on the course page in Moodle. Is it going to be this long-winded every time?

Don't worry! There are only two—at worst three—steps left. And although it seems to be a lot of effort the first time, it gets much quicker, as we move on. We are also trying to be organized from the start by putting our worksheets neatly into a folder, so we took a couple of extra steps that we won't have to do next time. The folder will already be there for us. Of course, you can just click on **Upload a file** and get your worksheets straight into the course files without any sort of order, and they will display for your students just as well. But when you have a lot of worksheets loaded, it will become harder and harder to locate them unless you have a system.

Time for action-displaying our factsheet on our course page

To get the Moodle course started, we need to create a link that—when clicked, will get the course started, carrying on from where we left off:

1. Click on the word **Choose** to the right of your worksheet. (We are **choosing** to put this on Moodle.)

2. The **River Thames** worksheet now shows in the **Location** box, under **Link to a file or web site**. We are almost there!

3. Scroll down and make sure that you have selected the **New window** option in the **Window** box, as shown in the following screenshot:

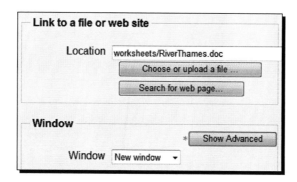

4. At the bottom of the screen, click on **Save** and return to course. Done!

 The option **Search for web page** would take you to Google or another search engine to find a web site. You could put that web site into the location box instead, and it would make a clickable link for your students to follow.

What just happened?

Congratulations! You've now made a link to the factsheet about the River Thames that will get our Rivers and Flooding course started! By doing the final step above, we will get taken back to the course page where we'll see the words that we wrote in the **Name** box. They'll be in blue with a line underneath. This tells us it's a clickable link that will take us to the factsheet. If you can do that once, you can do it many times.

Have a go hero-putting a slideshow onto Moodle

It's important to go through the steps again, pretty quickly, so that you become familiar with them and are able to speed the process up. So why not take one of your slide shows (maybe done in PowerPoint) and upload that to Moodle?

Start by creating a folder called `Slideshows`, so that in future, it will be available for any slideshows that you upload. Or, if you're too tired, just upload another sheet into our `Worksheets` folder and display that.

Putting a week's worth of slideshows into Moodle

Now let's suppose that we have already prepared a week's worth of slideshows. Actually, I could say, a month's worth of worksheets, or a year's worth of exam papers. Basically, what we're going to do is upload several items, all at once. This is very useful because once you get used to uploading and displaying worksheets, you will very quickly start thinking about how tedious it would be, to put them on Moodle one at a time. Especially if you are studying ten major world rivers, and you have to go through all of those steps ten times. Well, you don't!

Let's use my **River Processes** slideshows as our example. I have them saved in a folder on **My Computer** (as opposed to being shoved at random in a drawer, obviously!). Under normal circumstances, Moodle won't let you upload whole folders just like that. You have to either compress or zip them first (that basically means squeeze it up a bit, so it slides into cyberspace more smoothly).

We first need to leave Moodle for a while and go to our own computer. I'm using Windows; for Macs, it will be slightly different.

Time for action-getting a whole folder of work into Moodle in one go

To view the slideshows, we need to upload the folder containing them from the hard drive of our computer into Moodle.

1. Find the folder that you want to upload, right-click on it, and select **Compressed (zipped) Folder** within the **Send To** option.

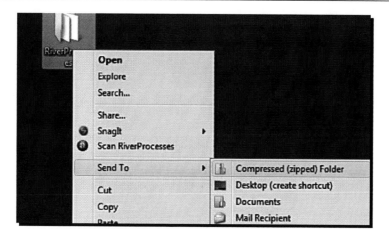

2. You'll get another folder with the same name, but in ZIP format.

3. Go to your Moodle course page, and in the **Administration** box, click **Files**.

 We're back in the course files storage area—recollect Chapter 1, and you'll remember that this is another way in, if you ever need one! You can upload anything straight into here, and then provide a link to a file or web site.

4. As we have done before, click on **Upload** and upload the zipped folder (it ends in `.zip`).

5. Now click on **Unzip**, which is displayed to the right of your folder name (as shown in the following screenshot), and the folder will be restored to its normal size.

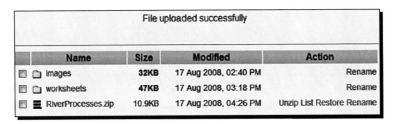

	Name	Size	Modified	Action
☐ 🗀	images	**32KB**	17 Aug 2008, 02:40 PM	Rename
☐ 🗀	worksheets	**47KB**	17 Aug 2008, 03:18 PM	Rename
☐ ▤	RiverProcesses.zip	10.9KB	17 Aug 2008, 04:26 PM	Unzip List Restore Rename

File uploaded successfully

What just happened?

We put a bunch of slideshows about how rivers work into a folder on our compter. We then **zipped** the folder to make it slide into Moodle, and then when it was uploaded, we unzipped it to get it back to normal.

If you want to be organized, select the checkbox displayed to the left of the zipped folder, and select **delete completely**. We don't need the zipped folder now, as we have got the original folder back.

We now have two choices. Using the **Link to a file or web site** option in the **Add a resource** block, we can display each slideshow, in an orderly manner, in the list. We did this with our Thames factsheet, so we know how to do this.

Alternatively, we can simply display the folder and let the students open it to get to the slideshows.

We're going to opt for the second choice. Why? Bearing in mind what was mentioned in Chapter 1 about appearances being vital, it would look much neater on our course page if we had a dinky little briefcase icon. The student can click on the briefcase icon to see the list of slideshows, rather than scrolling down a long list on the page. Let us see how this is done:

Time for action-displaying a whole folder on Moodle

Let us upload the entire folder, which contains the related slideshows, onto Moodle. This will require us to perform only four steps:

1. With editing turned on, click on **Add a resource** and choose **Display a directory**.

2. In the **Name** field, type something meaningful for the students to click on and add a description in the **Summary** field, if you wish.

3. Click on **Display a directory** and find the one that you want—for us, **RiverProcesses**.

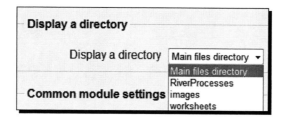

4. Scroll down, and click on **Save and return to course**.

What just happened?

We made a link to a week's worth of slideshows on our course page, instead of displaying them one at a time. If we looked at the outcome, instead of the icon of a slideshow, such as the Powerpoint icon, we get a folder icon. When the text next to it is clicked, the folder opens, and all of the slideshows inside can be viewed. It is much easier on the eye, when you go directly to the course page, than going through a long list of stuff.

> 📁 Slideshows about River Processes

Making a 'click here' type link to the River Thames web site

Let's learn how to create a link that will lead us to the River Thames web site, or in fact to any web site. However, we're investigating the Thames at the moment, so this would be really helpful. Just imagine, how much simpler it would be for our students to be able to get to a site in one click, rather than type it by hand, spell it wrong, and have it not work. We already learned one way to do this in Chapter 1. The way we will learn now is easier. In fact, it's so easy that you could do it yourself with only one hint from me.

Have a go hero-linking to a web site

Do you recollect that we uploaded our worksheet and used **Link to a file or web site**? We linked it to a file (our worksheet). Here, you just need to link to a web site, and everything else is just the same. When you get to the **Link to a file or web site** box, instead of clicking **Choose or upload a file...**, just type in, or copy and paste, the web site that you want to link to (making sure you include only one `http://`). Remember that we saw earlier, that if you click on **Search for web page...**, it will take you to Google or some other **Seach Engine** web page to find you a web site that you'd like to link to.

The following screenshot shows how to link a file or web site into our Moodle course:

That's it! Try it! Go back to your course page; click on the words that you specified as the **Name** for the web page link, and check whether it works. It should open the web page in a new window, so that once finished, our students can click on the **X** to close the site and will still have Moodle running in the background.

Recap—where do we stand now?

We have learnt a lot of interesting things so far. Lets just have a recap of the things that we have learned so far. We have learnt to:

- Upload and display individual worksheets (as we've worked on the River Thames)
- Upload and display whole folders of worksheets (as we did with the River Processes slideshows folder)
- Make a **click here** type link to any web site that we want, so that our students will just need to click on this link to get to that web site

We're now going to have a break from filling up our course for a while, and take a step to another side. Our first venture into Moodle's features was the **Link to a file or web site** option, but there are many more yet to be investigated. Let's have a closer look at those **Add a resource...** options in the following screenshot, so that we know, where we are heading:

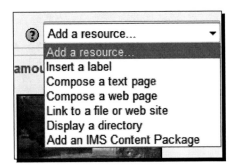

The table below shows all of the **Add a Resource...** options. What are they, which is the one we need, and what can we safely ignore? You might recognize one or two already. We shall meet the others in a moment.

Item	What it is	Do we need it?
Insert a label	A bit of white space to separate resources on the page	Yes—it improves the appearance of the course page
Compose a text page	Space to type straight into Moodle (and do more advanced stuff)	Could do, but we will use web pages instead
Compose a web page	As above, but with more options	Yes—we can do our worksheets directly in Moodle
Link to a file or web site	Shows our worksheet or a web site	Yes—we use it all the time
Display a directory	Shows a whole folder of work	Yes—makes the course page neater
Add an IMS content package	A place to upload special types of resources (for advanced users)	No—but if you're curious, you can check out the web site, `http://www.udutu.com`

Creating a worksheet about flooding, directly in Moodle

Now, this is progress. At the start of the chapter, we had barely learned how to upload what we already had, and now we are thinking of typing straight into Moodle. But hold on—why should we bother? We're pretty proficient in MS Word, and with each upload we do, we take less time to do it.

Recollect the introduction, where I had said that this chapter was about saving energy—ours and the world's. Actually, it can also be about saving the children's energy, and even avoiding their frustration. If we go back to our course page and click on one of our worksheets, what happens? Depending on the browser that is being used—in this case **Internet Explorer (IE)**—we get a pop-up dialog box, as shown in the following screenshot:

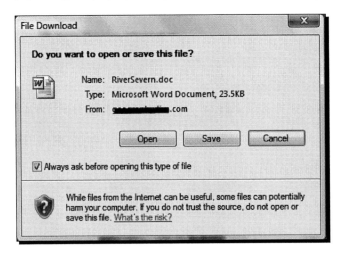

Here, having already clicked on the link, we are being asked to make a choice between three options. If we choose **Open**, we will have to wait for a while, for the file to open. So that's two clicks and a wait. For a ten-year old, or even younger, that's a long time to wait, and the novelty will soon wear off once the kid's done that half a dozen times, once for each of our river's worksheets. Additionally, not all children have Microsoft Office installed (as we are going to see later, in Chapter 8), but they can all click a link on the Internet. Thus, can we not just have one click, and no wait?

Yes! If we type our worksheet straight into Moodle, as we're about to do. The next stage of our unit of work is to research the major floods that took place in the tiny Cornish village of Boscastle in 2004. Instead of wasting time typing a worksheet out and then uploading it, let's just do it in Moodle straight away, and cut out that middle step!

Time for action-typing our flooding worksheet straight into Moodle

We have already learned how to create worksheets and upload a folder containing them into Moodle. Let's now try to create the worksheets in Moodle, directly.

1. With editing turned on, go to **Add a resource**, and click on **Compose a web page**.

2. In the **Name** field, type the text that the students will have to click on to access the page. Then, scroll down to compose a web page, as shown in the following screenshot:

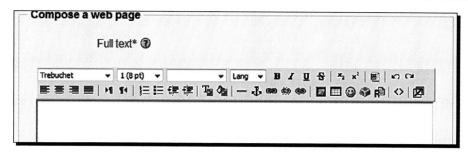

3. Type in the instructions, as you would have done it in Microsoft Word, or a similar software application.

4. Use the toolbar in the HTML editor to change the font size, color, and add images, according to your choice.

5. Make sure that the **Window** option is set to **New window**.

6. Click on **Save** and return to course.

Wasn't that easy? We got the outcome in just four steps, in comparison to the 17 steps that were needed when we first uploaded and displayed our River Thames worksheet. Our outcome of the Flooding worksheet will appear as shown in the following screenshot. I've included hyperlinks because we are allowed to do that in Moodle. It took me only a couple of minutes.

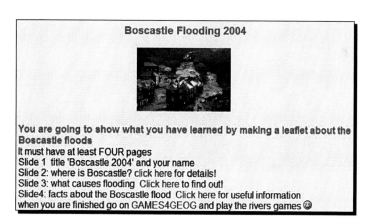

Make sure that you **save your work regularly**! At the moment, Moodle doesn't automatically save your work. Until it starts doing that, it's best to do it yourself, so that you don't need to begin all over again if your Internet connection goes down.

What just happened?

We have now created our first worksheet directly in Moodle, without the need to create it offline first, and then upload it onto Moodle. If we go back to our course page and click on the words we used as the name for the **link**, we get to see the instructions in just one click. Students will thank you for this, and you will be glad that you didn't have to type it out first, then upload it, and finally link to it!

Don't think of a web page as something only geek web designers need to use. In Moodle, it is simply a space you can type into, just like each topic summary.

Online worksheets—some ideas to consider

I hope you can see that although being able to display a years' worth of worksheets and slideshows (which is a very powerful feature of Moodle) is useful, it can often be simpler and friendlier to create the task directly in Moodle. If you've already prepared a worksheet, for example in MS Word, you can also copy and paste it (although it doesn't always display exactly the same as your original).

If you are lucky enough to have a projector, a whiteboard, and an Internet connection in your room, why not present your instructions to your class on a web page in Moodle, instead of writing them by hand? You can then plan the course in advance and show it through your projector when you are ready.

If you have a homework task that does not involve the class having to download and take print outs of your worksheet, why not make that a web page?

If you can get your class into a computer room, why not have them view your web page on their own computers and follow the instructions there? These days, many schools are moving towards using cute little mini-books and laptops for each child. We could well see Moodle as the **virtual** online exercise book of the future! You could use the hyperlinking facility to great advantage if you want them to do some research on a particular topic and need to guide them to specific areas. You direct them to the most useful web sites, they click on your links, and are on their! This is particularly helpful for younger children who need clear direction rather than simply "go to Google and research...".

Be careful that you avoid the usage of plain black text and long instructions. Use different colors and brighten the page up with an image (we looked at the display of images in Chapter 1).

Making our page look prettier

Is this really important? Shouldn't we be getting on with all of the other activities that Moodle can offer? Yes we should, and we shall, but it is vital that we make our course page appeal to the students. I cannot stress this enough. We have looked at this in Chapter 1 when we set our course up, and now that we've got topics with worksheets, folders, hyperlinks, and web pages that are starting to fill the screen space, it's worth looking at it again. We really need to ensure that our classes don't just take one look and run. Long pages of writing are sure to turn the users off. How do you think the users might react to a Moodle page that appears as shown in the following screenshot?

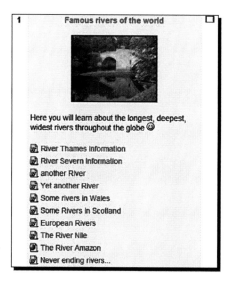

Even though it looks like a nice picture, the arrangement of the worksheets doesn't seem very pleasant to the eyes. We can do two things to improve it:

1. Put them into a folder and show only that folder (**display a directory**).
    Add a bit of white space between the worksheets to separate them, categorise them (and—of course—give them more descriptive titles rather than 'another river' and so on!)

2. We already know how to do the first option (but we must be careful, once we get loads of content in our course, that we don't just have long lists of directories instead of individual worksheets). So let's try the second option—the white space. We'll be using the Label that we saw in that table I made earlier.

Time for action-improving the look of our course page

Currently, our course page doesn't look very pleasant to the eye. Let's make it a little more interesting.

1. With editing turned on, go to **Add a resource** and choose **Insert a label**.

2. Type in some text in order to separate or categorize a number of worksheets.

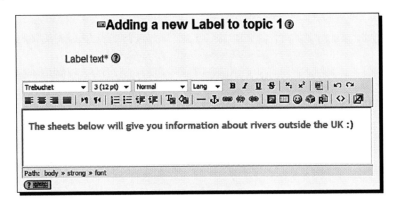

3. Finally, click on **Save** and return to course.

What just happened?

We added a description of the worksheets in the provided white space known as **Label**. It seems to be very nice, but the description has appeared underneath the names of the rivers when we wanted it in between. Check out the icons next to each of the resources when editing is turned on. They all have an important role to play in editing the material on our page.

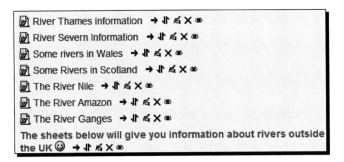

One of the listed icons will enable us to move the label to where we want it (by default, every time you add a resource on a Moodle page, it goes under the previous one). Here is a table that briefly explains what each icon does. Look out for the one that will move our label up.

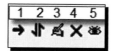

Icon	What it is	Why do we need it?
1	Indents to the right	For subsections/subheadings
2	Moves up or down	Very useful (you might have a drag/drop handlebar icon instead)
3	Editing text	Essential for setting up/altering resources
4	Delete	Deletes from a page, not a course
5	Hides item (click to close the eye; click again to re-open)	Very useful for showing an item only when you want to

Now, what we need is the arrows going up or down. You might have a handlebar icon on your Moodle instead. In this case, you gently drag-and-drop your item to where you want it.

Have a go hero-move the label

Just click on the up or down arrow next to the label. Don't panic if it vanishes—it's just hovering in cyberspace, waiting to be moved to your preferred location. Click on one of the empty boxes as shown in the following screenshot, and the label will move there.

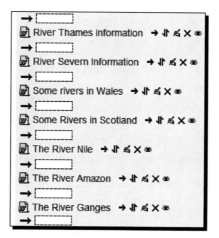

Incidentally, we aren't tied to moving stuff within a topic area. We can move from one topic section to another and, in fact, use the arrows to the right of each topic section to move entire topics up and down.

You can get a preview of how our course page will appear to the student. There's a useful box at the top of the screen, next to the editing button, called **Switch role to**. If you click on it and choose **Student**, it temporarily lets you see the page as the child would see it. Our latest effort would appear as shown in the following screenshot:

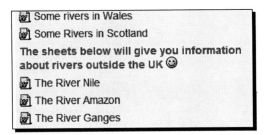

Summary

In this chapter, we've started assembling work for our classes in Moodle. We've looked at saving time and energy by:

♦ Getting individual worksheets into Moodle for our students (so we don't have to keep printing them)

♦ Getting whole folders of work into Moodle (instead of uploading them one at a time)

♦ Making quick and easy links to web sites

♦ Creating a worksheet from scratch in Moodle, instead of doing this offline and then uploading the worksheet

Additionally, we've also provided tips on improving the appearance of the course by:

♦ Showing work in a folder instead of showing everything separately in a list

♦ Breaking up the work into chunks by using a label

♦ Moving items around the page

Setting up this web page was just the beginning. If we can do that, it's only one tiny step further to getting our students to learn interactively and to send us their work within Moodle. That's where we're heading in the next chapter.

3
Getting Interactive

Congratulations on reaching the Chapter 3! Some people choose never to go beyond the skills acquired in Chapters 1 and 2, and are then surprised when their Moodle course doesn't really take off with the students or their colleagues. In the following pages, we shall reach into the heart of Moodle. The previous chapters were about what we could do for our children. This one is about what they can give back to us!

This chapter combines classroom tasks with Moodle activities, in a mini-project that will get our students to think and collaborate. We'll also add a competitive element to it and—just as we have seen on TV—let the children vote for the winner. The tasks we set will involve the students researching, collaborating, and reflecting. They will be working hard, but we'll have a much easier time now, as all of their responses will be on Moodle for us to view and mark at our convenience—no more carrying heavy books around.

We are going to carry out a role-play activity. This activity will be geography-based, but the Moodle activities are the same for any subject. Hopefully, this will help you gain some ideas for your own teaching. Having learned about the course of a river and about the landscape at the location where the river meets the coast, the students are now going to be given the job of developers—planning and designing a riverside campsite. The students will undertake various tasks during the project, all of them within Moodle. We, the teachers, having set the scene, are going to sit back and observe their progress, online. When the entire mini-project is complete, we're going to get them to tell us, personally, how much they feel they have learned. We can use their responses to plan our future Moodle activities.

In this chapter, we shall encourage our students to join in by:

- Allowing them to discuss the considerations in choosing the location of this campsite in a safe, moderated **forum**
- Giving them an out-of-school hours **chatroom** in which they can plan their site
- Asking them to suggest creative names for the site and entering these names in a class **glossary**
- Providing a space (in a **database**) to send in their designs for the teacher to assess and their classmates to view
- Letting the class vote on the winner and evaluating the project by using a Moodle **choice**
- Getting them to send in their advert for us to mark directly within Moodle as an **assignment**
- Having them tell a story to which everyone can contribute by using a **Wiki**

How do we do all this?

The words in **bold** above are examples of activities that we can do in Moodle. There are others too, but for you—as a newbie—these seven activities are more than enough. To set up any of them, we first need to turn editing on, either via the button on the upper right of the screen, or via the **Administration** block. Then, in the topic section where we want to add our activity, we click on the space next to **Add an activity...**. This will bring up a list of options, which might vary depending upon your particular Moodle course. The following screenshot shows some typical options that might show up when you click **Add an activity...**. Be aware that **Certificate** and **Game** don't appear in standard Moodle courses, but I shall elaborate more on this topic in the final chapter.

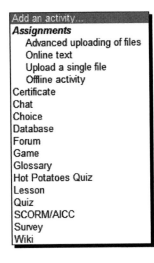

Getting our class to reflect and discuss

Have you ever come across a child who is too shy to speak up in class but then produces the most thoughtful written work? Moodle is Godsend for these students, because it has a forum and a chat facility, both of which enable classes and their teachers to have a discussion without actually being together, in the same room. And often, the shy child will happily have their say online, where they can plan it out first and feel comfortable without the interference of their peers. We're going to set some homework where the students will discuss, in general, the kinds of things to keep in mind when planning a riverside campsite. Hopefully, someone will realize it's not a good idea to have it too close to the water.

Time for action-setting up a discussion forum on Moodle

Let's create an online discussion area for the students to share their views and comments. This discussion area is called the **Forum**.

1. With editing turned on, click on **Add an activity** and select **Forum**. As a result, the following information will appear on the screen.

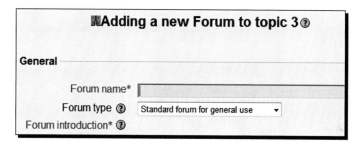

2. In the **Forum type** field, click on the drop-down arrow and choose **Single Simple Discussion** (we'll investigate on the other options later).

3. In the **Forum name** field, enter some text that will invite your students to click on it to join the discussion.

4. In the **Message** field, enter your starting topic, with images and hyperlinks, if you wish.

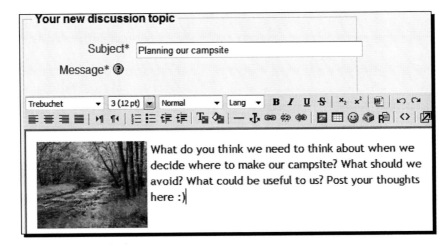

5. Change the option **Force everyone to be subscribed** to **Yes**, if you want people to get an email every time somebody adds their comments or suggestions to the forum.

6. Leave the option **Read tracking** as it is, and people can decide whether to track read or unread messages.

7. The option, **Maximum attachment size** lets you decide how big a file or an image people can attach with a message.

8. Grade—alter these settings to give each post a mark. But be aware that this will put younger children off.

9. You can put a number in the **Post threshold for blocking** option if you want to limit the number of posts that a student can make.

10. Click on **Save** and return to course.

What just happened?

We have just set up an online discussion area (forum) on a specific topic for our class. Let's go back to our course page and click on the forum that we just prepared. The final output will look like this:

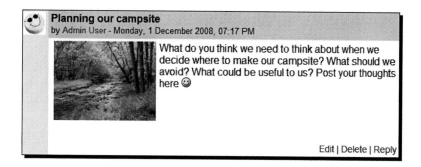

Our students will see an icon (usually with two faces) that will prompt them to join the preliminary discussion on where best to locate the campsite. They'll click on the **Reply** link at the bottom (as you can see in the preceding screenshot), to post their response.

How do we moderate the forum?

Hopefully, we can just read the students' responses and let them discuss the topic amongst themselves. But as a teacher, we do have three other options:

1. We can edit the response posted by the student (change the wording if it's inappropriate).
2. We can delete the post altogether.
3. We can reply to it when we think it is really important to do so.

A student only has the option to reply (as you see if you click on **Student view** at the upper right of the course page). When we need to get rid of an unsuitable post, or perhaps alter the wording of something one of our students has typed, this extra power we teachers have is helpful.

For our **starter** discussion, we chose a Single Simple Discussion as we wanted the students to focus totally on one issue. However, in other situations, you might need a slightly different type of forum. So the following table gives a brief overview of the other kinds that are available, and explains how you could use them:

Name	What it does	Why use it
Single Simple Discussion	Only one question students can all answer	Best for focused discussions – students can't get distracted
Standard forum	Everyone can start a new topic	More scope for older students
Q and A	Pupils must answer first before they can see any replies	Useful for avoiding peer pressure issues
Each person posts 1 discussion	Pupils can post ONE new topic only	Handy if you need to restrict posting but still allow some freedom

Why use a forum?

Here are a few other thoughts on forums, based on my own experiences:

- A cross-year or cross-class forum can be useful, as the older students can pass on their experiences to the younger students. For example, each year my first year high school students make a volcano as a homework project. As they enter their second year, they use a dedicated forum to pass on their wisdom and answer technical questions sought by the inexperienced first-year students—who are about to begin their own creations.

- A homework exercise could be set on a forum, as a reflective plenary to the learning done in the class. Once, my class watched a documentary based on the Great New Orleans flood of 2004, and the students were asked, on a forum, to imagine they had been there. They had to suggest some words or phrases to describe their feelings—which we then collated into the next lesson to make poems about the flood.

- Let's add a little bit of confusion. Instead of simply asking a question, why not make a statement that you know will inspire, annoy, and divide the students. As a result, you can see the variety in the responses. I once posted the topic: "If people live near rivers, and their homes get flooded out, it is surely their own fault for living near rivers. Why should the rest of us have to help them?" In response to this, some violently disagreed with the statement—quoting examples from developing countries, whereas some agreed with the statement—and were then blasted down by their classmates for doing so. But at least the forum got visited!

Carrying on the conversation in real time—outside of school

A discussion forum, as illustrated above, is a useful tool to get the children to think and to contribute their ideas. It has an advantage over the usual class discussion, in that the shyer pupils are more likely to open up in such discussion forums. However, there is no spontaneity involved. You might post a comment in the morning, and the response may arrive at dinner time, and so on. Why not combine the advantages of online communication with the advantages of a real time conversation, and make a **Moodle chat room**? If your students live several miles away from each other, as my students do, and are keen to get on with the project, Moodle chat rooms can have real benefits. We can set a time for the chat—say, Saturday afternoon. This would be a time when we can be present too, if we wish, and the students can move ahead with their plans even though they're not with each other in the classroom. Even though this implementation has its own drawbacks, it provides us with a set-up. Eventually, we can see how it goes and then think about how best we can use it.

Time for action-setting up a chat room in Moodle

Let's create a chat room where the students can have a chat even when they are not in the same classroom. This way, they can share their views, comments, and suggestions.

1. With editing turned on, go to **Add an activity**, and select the **Chat** option.

2. In the **Name of this chat room** field, enter an appropriate title for the discussion.

3. In the **Introduction text** field, type in what the discussion is going to be about.

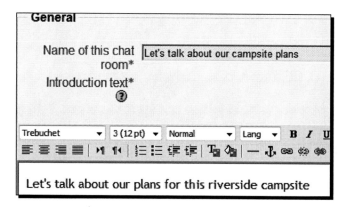

4. For the **Next chat time** option, choose when you want to open the chat room.

5. For the **Repeat sessions** option, choose whether you want to chat regularly, or just once.

6. For the **Save past sessions** option, choose how long, if at all, to keep a record of the conversation.

7. It is up to you to decide whether to allow everyone to view the past sessions or not.

8. For now, you can ignore the **Common module settings** option.

9. Click on **Save and Display**.

What just happened?

We have set up the place and time on Moodle for our students to talk to each other—and even with us if necessary—online. Students will see an icon—usually a speech bubble—on the course page, alongside the name given to the chat. The students just have to click on the icon at the correct time for the chat. When the room is open, they will see this:

Clicking on the link will take the students to a box where they'll be able to see their user photo (if they have one) and the time at which they have entered the chat. When others join in, their photos will be shown, and the time of their arrival will be recorded. You **talk** by typing into the long box at the bottom of the screen, and when submitted, your words appear in the larger box above it. This can get quite confusing if a lot of people are typing at the same time, as the contributions appear one under the other, and do not always follow on from the question or response to which they are referring.

Why use Chat? (and why not?)

I have to confess that I have switched off the ability for people to use **Chat** on my school's Moodle site. Chat does have one advantage over the **Forum**, which is that you can hold discussions in real time with the others who are not physically present in the same room as you. This could be useful on occasions, such as when the teacher is absent from school (but available online). He or she can contact the class at the start of the lesson to check whether they know what they are doing. The students in our school council use **Chat** for meetings out of school hours, as do our school Governors. You can also read the transcript of a chat (the **chat log**) after it has happened. However, everyone really has to stay focused on the discussion topic, otherwise, you risk having nothing but a list of trite comments, and no real substance. I've found this to be the case with younger children. Personally, I find a single and a simple discussion in a **Forum** to be of much more value, than **Chat**. However, you can try using Chat and see what you think. Your experience could be different from mine.

Making our own class Glossary

Finally, the thinking part is over; now it's time to get started. Our campsite needs a name, and thirty heads are better than one. The next task will have the students suggesting interesting names for the site and the reasons why they think that their name should be chosen.

For this, we are going to use a **Glossary**, which is similar to an online dictionary. The only difference is that it is you (or the students) who adds all the information into the Glossary. You can add single words, phrases, or even images to a glossary. You can even set it up in such a way that when you use one of the keywords in your course, Moodle automatically makes a link to the entry for that word in the glossary. The students can then click on these links to learn more about them. Glossaries are useful for teachers who want to provide key terms for a particular topic, but students learn best from them when they build up the vocabulary themselves. We're going to get our students to add possible names for the riverside site to a Glossary. We want the students to think creatively and imaginatively, and to justify their choices.

Time for action-getting students to create their own Glossary

Let's create a **Glossary** where the students will be able post their suggestions. This will help us in understanding their choices.

1. With editing turned on, select the **Glossary** option, within the **Add an activity** option.

2. Provide a suitable name for the glossary in the **Name** field, and describe what the glossary's about in the **Description** text block.

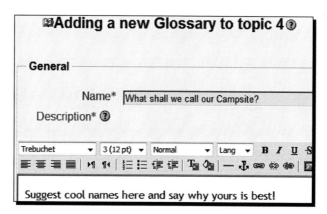

3. There are many options that you can specify for a glossary. To start with, just leave them as they are shown in the following screenshot:

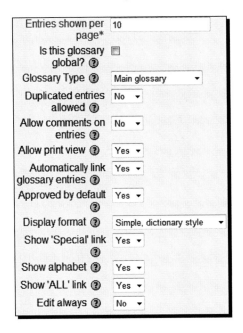

 If you want to moderate entries before they appear in the glossary, choose **No** in the **Approved by default** field. If you want to let students comment on entries, choose **Yes** in the **Allow comments box**.

4. Click on **Save and display**.

What just happened?

We've set up an area on Moodle where our class students can add their suggested names for the campsite. We're using a **Glossary** which we could—under other circumstances—use as a collaborative dictionary, giving our students the task of building it up, and saving ourselves the effort. If we look at the finished article now, it will appear as shown in the following screenshot:

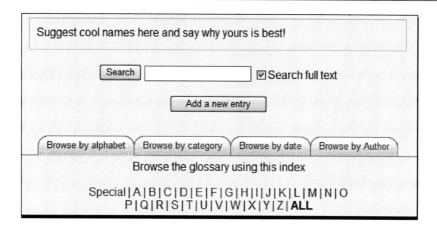

- In order to enter a word, or suggested campsite name, into the glossary click on **Add a new entry**
- In the **Concept** field, enter your word or term–in our case, the suggested campsite name
- In the **Description** field, enter the definition of the glossary term—in our case, the reasoning behind the choice of name

Don't be put off by all the tabs. As you get more into Moodle, you can investigate the glossary further. You can set categories for entries. For example, you can add keywords, that is, synonyms, that will be hyperlinked to our glossary terms wherever they appear in our course. We could also set a rating system for the glossary and allow our students to give points to the most popular names. For now, however, we just want our class to add words.

Showcasing the plans in a database

Let's assume that the students have decided on the campsite location and design. The students can make use of Microsoft Paint or OpenOffice Draw to draw and label their plans. They have to save their work as a .jpg file—in other words, as an image ready to be shared with others. We now need a space on Moodle where the students can send in their plans for others to see and to vote for. In this case, a Moodle **database** will serve our purpose well. Don't be put off by the term database. Being a non-technical person myself, the term database conjures up visions of spreadsheets and formulae to me. In Moodle, the database is merely a communal area where anyone can upload items or add information for others to view. However, as with the glossary, the Moodle database has a lot of extra features that we don't need yet—so we'll just ignore them.

Time for action-setting up a database

Let's create a database to which the students can post their designs.

1. With editing turned on, select the **Database** option within the **Add an Activity** option.

2. In the **Name** field, provide a suitable title for your database and, in the **Introduction** block, specify what you want the students to add—in our case, the image file of their campsite design.

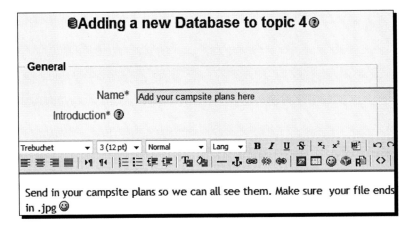

3. Don't worry about any settings that you're not sure of. For now, just click on **Save and Display**.

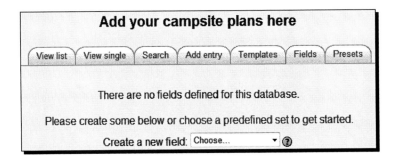

4. Click on the drop-down arrow for the **Create a new field** field, and select **Picture**, as shown in the following screenshot.

 Fields are simply bits of information, such as names, addresses, dates, and so on.

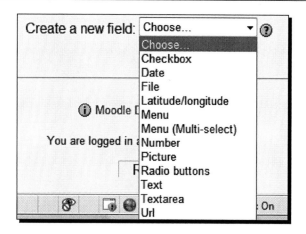

5. In the **Field Name** field, enter a suitable title for the field and in the **Field Description** field, enter what you want the student to do (such as upload their campsite design). Set the image size, if you wish, by entering a width and height in pixels next to the **Width** and **Height** fields.

6. Click on **Add**, and then select **text area**.

7. Fill in the appropriate details, as shown in the following screenshot, setting a width and height for the text field depending on the amount of text that you want the students to enter (you might need to experiment with an optimum text box size).

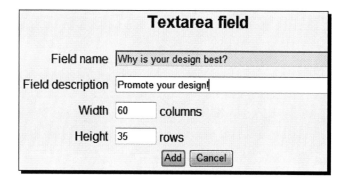

8. Click on the **Add** button to save.

What just happened?

We set up an area—a database—in Moodle with space for our students to send in their plans, and space for them to **sell** us their designs. If we look at our finished activity, we will see this:

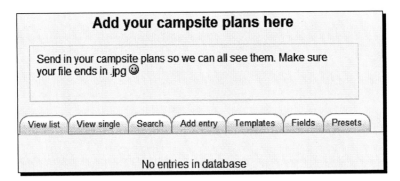

Clicking on the **Add entry** tab will take us—and our students—to the upload area, as shown in the following screenshot:

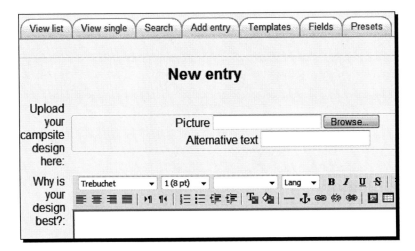

Now, we need to wait until all the designs are in. Let's take a break for a moment.

How far have we come?

The aim of this chapter was to get our students involved—as our Teaching Assistant—in a project with Moodle. So far, they've made use of the **Forum** and the **Chat** room to exchange their initial thoughts and ideas. They've come up with the names for the site, which they've shared in a glossary, and also come up with the actual design, which they have uploaded to a database. They weren't tied to working in the classroom or during school hours. They didn't even need to be sitting side by side with their classmates to discuss. Just imagine—the students have set up the tasks, and they didn't even need us—the teachers—to be there (although it's important to keep an eye on their discussions). This is another attraction of Moodle; students can work independently, once they have understood what is to be done. However, one thing that Moodle cannot do is choose the best campsite design (although, it can mark many other activities for us—as we shall see in Chapter 4). Now, that we are done with our short break, let's add an option to our course page that enables our class to pick the winner.

Giving our class a chance to vote

Moodle has an activity, known as **Choice,** which allows you to present students with a number of options that they can choose from. We're actually going to use it twice in our project, for two different purposes. Let's us try and set it up.

Time for action-giving students a chance to choose a winner

The students have posted their suggestions, comments, and views on Moodle. A choice is to be made of the best suggestion. Who better, than the students themselves to choose and vote for the best?

1. With editing turned on, click on **Add an Activity** and then select **Choice.**

2. In the **Name** field, enter an appropriate descriptive text—in our case, this is **Vote for the best design here.**

3. In the **Choice Text** field, ask the question based on which you want the students to cast a vote.

4. Leave the **Limit** field as it is if you don't mind any number of students casting a vote for any option available. Change it to **enable**, if you only want a certain number of people to vote for a particular choice. We shall leave the **Limit** block as it is, but we shall inform the students that they can't vote for themselves.

5. In the **Choice** block, type in the options (a minimum of two) you want the students to be able to cast their vote for. Clicking on **Add more fields** will provide you with more choice boxes. We will need one field for each member of the class, for this activity.

6. Use the **Restrict answering to this time period** option to decide when to open and close your **Choice**—or have it always available.

7. **Miscellaneous settings:** For our activity, we need to set **Display Mode** to **Vertical** set and **Publish Results** to **Do Not Publish**. The following table explains what the settings mean, so you can use them on other occasions.

Setting	What it is	Why use it
Display Mode	Lets you have your buttons go across or down the screen	Use **Vertically** if you have many options, to avoid stretching your screen
Publish Results	Decide if and when you want students to see what others have specified	Choose **Do not publish** if you want students to tell you their progress privately; if you're doing a class survey, for example, choose **Always show results**
Privacy of Results	Lets you choose whether to show names or not	Are the results more important than who voted for what? Some students might be wary of responding if they think their names will be shown
Allow choice to be updated	Lets students change their mind—but they can still vote only once	Useful, if you are using this to assess progress over a period of time
Show column for unanswered	Sets up a column showing those who haven't yet responded	A clear visual way of knowing who hasn't done the task

8. For now, you can ignore the **Common Module Settings** option, and just click on **Save and return to course.**

What just happened?

We've set up an area, on our course page, where the students can choose their favorite designs from a number of options, by clicking on the desired option button. On the screen, you will be able to see an icon (usually, a question mark) and some text next to it. If you click on the text next to the icon, the following information will appear:

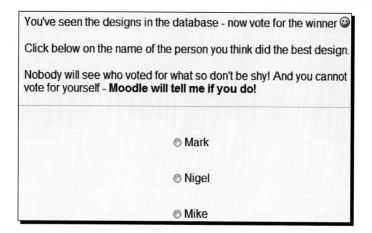

The students will click on the option button placed next to their choice—in our case, the name of the classmate whose design they prefer.

Finding out the students' choice

1. Access the **Choice** option and click on the words **View *** responses** on the upper right of the screen.The *** will be the number of students who have voted already.

2. You will get a chart displaying the choices of the students. In my Moodle course, as shown in the following screenshot, nobody has voted yet—so they need a gentle nudge!

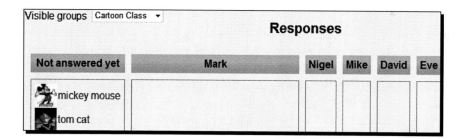

Remember that we have set up this activity so that our students cannot see the results, in order to avoid peer pressure or bullying. However, *we* can see the results. Thus, if Mickey votes for himself (even after having been told not to) we will spot it and can reprimand him.

Have a go hero-getting the class to give us feedback

After we've gone through all of the effort to set up our project on Moodle, it would be nice to know how well it was received. Why not go off now and set up another **Choice** option, where the question asks **how much did you enjoy planning & designing the campsite?** You could give them three simple responses (displayed horizontally) as:

1. A lot.
2. It was OK.
3. Not very much.

Or you could be more specific, focusing on the individual activities and asking how much they feel they have benefited from, say, the wiki or the forum. Make sure it is set up, so that the students don't see the results—that way they're more likely to be truthful.

Why use Choice?

Here are a few other thoughts on **Choice**, based on my own experiences:

- It is a fast and simple method of gathering data for a class research project. I used this with a class of 13 year olds who had just returned from the summer break. I asked them to choose where they had been on vacation, giving them choices of our own country, several nearby countries in Europe, the United States of America, and a few more. I set up the choice, so that they could all see the answers when the time was up. I also set it up in such a way that the results were anonymous, to avoid any kind of uneasiness felt by those students who had stayed at home. The class then compared and contrasted the class results with Tourist Office statistics on the most popular tourist destinations.

- It offers a private way for students to evaluate and inform the teacher about their progress. Students might be too shy to tell you in person if they are struggling; they might be wary of being honest in the open voting methods that some teachers use (such as red, amber, or green traffic lights). However, if the students are aware of the fact that their classmates will not see their response, they are more likely to be honest with you.

- It acts as a way to involve the class in deciding the path that their learning will take. I first introduced my class of 11 year olds to rivers in Europe, South America, Africa, and Asia. Then, I offered the class, the chance to vote for the river that they wanted study in greater depth as part of their project. The majority opted for the Amazon—so the Amazon it was!

Announcing the winner

Well, you could give out the results in the classroom, of course! Alternatively, can encourage them to use Moodle by using the Compose a Webpage resource that we met in the previous chapter, and adding the information there.

Writing creatively in Moodle

Once a winner has been found, the next task for everyone is to create a cleverly-worded advertisement for this campsite, for which, you could use one of the names suggested in the glossary. This too can be done on Moodle. Why use Moodle and not their exercise books? The first reason is that it will save paper, the second reason is that the students **enjoy** working on the computer, and the third and final reason is that we can work at our leisure in school, at home, or in any room where there is an Internet connection. We're not tied to carrying around a pile of heavy books. We don't even need to manually hand-write the grades into our grade book. Moodle will put the grades that we give our students, into its grade book automatically and alphabetically. Moodle can also send our pupils an email telling them that we've graded their task, so that they can check their grades. This might be a different way of working from the one that you are used to, but do give it a try. It will take the pressure off your back and shoulders, if nothing else.

Time for action-setting up an online creative writing exercise

For our advert, we'll use an **Online text** assignment. We'll have a look at the others, afterwards.

1. With editing turned on, select **online text** option, within **Assignments.**

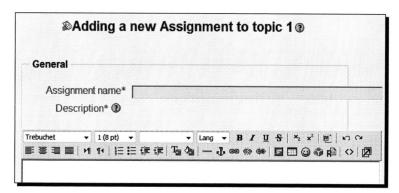

2. In the **Assignment name** field, enter something descriptive—our students will click here to get to the task.

3. In the **Description** field, enter the instructions. Our screen will then appear as shown in the following screenshot:

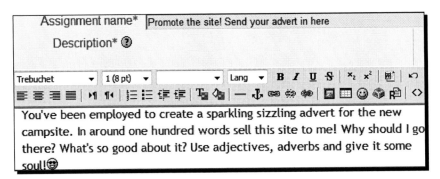

If you need more space to type in, click on the icon on the far right of the bottom line of the HTML editor. This will enlarge the text box for you. Click it again when you're done, to return to the editing area.

4. In the **Grade** field, enter the total marks out of which you will score the students (for now, we're sticking to a maximum of 100, but you can change this).

5. Set a start and end date between which the students can send the work assigned to them, if you want.

6. Leave the **Prevent Late Submissions** option as it is, unless you need to set a deadline by which the students must submit the assigned work.

7. Set the **Allow Resubmitting** option to **YES,** if you want to let students redraft their work.

8. Set the **Email Alerts to teachers** option to **NO** (unless you want 30 emails in your inbox!).

9. Change the **Comment inline** option to **YES,** so that we can post a comment on the students work.

10. Click on **Save** and return to course.

What just happened?

We've just explained to our class what we want them to do, and have also provided them with space in Moodle to do it. We used an **Online Text** assignment.

If we go up to the top of our course, where the editing button is, you'll be able to see a very useful feature called **Switch role to...**. If we choose the **Student** option, it will allow us to see the tasks as the pupils will see them:

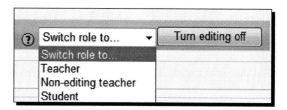

In this case, there's a rather unfriendly command at the bottom of our assignment. Do you think that your students will know that they need to click here to get to their text box?

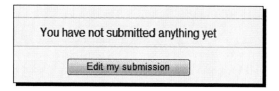

Why not ask your Moodle administrator to look at the Language editing settings and change these words to something more child-friendly—such as **Click here to type your answer**?

Marking students' work on Moodle

Now that the students have done their bit, it's time that we did ours. The difference is that, instead of staying late after school or taking a pile of exercise books home and then searching around for a red pen (or green, as in my school) we can just type our comment on top of their entry. If we go back to the assignment and click on it, we'll see a message on the upper right of the screen, as shown in the following screenshot:

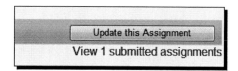

The number displayed on the screen is the number of children who've completed the task. If we click on this link, we'll be transported into Moodle's online grade book, as shown in the following screenshot:

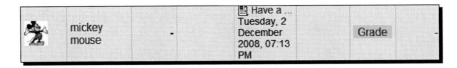

Eventually, after clicking on the link, we will be able to see whose work it is (Mickey Mouse, in our case). Moodle has also recorded the time at which the student posted it, and will also record the time that we (the teacher) grade the post. We need to click on **Grade** on the right and get our online pen ready. By doing this, we'll be able to see a window similar to the one shown in the following screenshot:

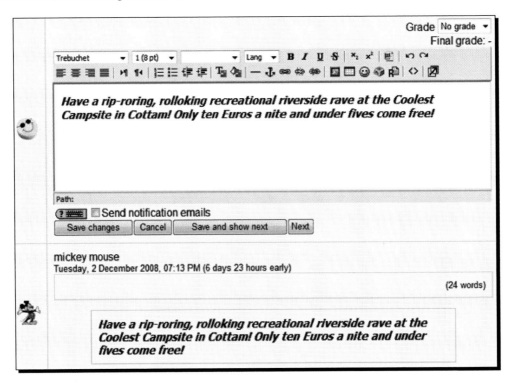

The student's effort is shown at the bottom of the screen—but it's also present in our HTML editor box. So, we can correct the student's words but will still keep the original for him to compare against. Moodle also tells us how many words the student has written (in our case, **24 words**). I have made it clear that I wanted the suggestion to be 100 words, so that's lost him some marks already.

We can type a general comment, ahead of Mickey's work, using a different color to separate our work from his. We can then use the features of the HTML editor to highlight, cross out, or even underline errors, depending on our personal marking style.

We can then select a suitable grade in the box at the top and, if we want, ensure that he gets an email telling him that his work has been awarded a grade. Before we save, let's just look at the corrected version. It will look similar to what is shown in the following screenshot:

If we have lots to mark, we can click on **Save and show next**, which will take us to the next post in our register, posted by a student. Let's just click **Save changes** for now.

What just happened?

We have just finished grading the students on their very first exercise in Moodle! The grade book was waiting there for us. We saw that **mickey mouse** had sent in his work. Thus, we clicked on **Grade** and were able to correct it, comment on it, and give it a grade. By saving our corrections, we've now added them to the grade book and can see how this looks in the following screenshot:

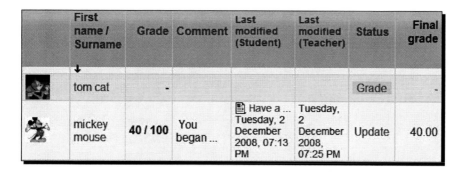

	First name / Surname	Grade	Comment	Last modified (Student)	Last modified (Teacher)	Status	Final grade
	↓						
	tom cat		-			Grade	-
	mickey mouse	40 / 100	You began ...	📄 Have a ... Tuesday, 2 December 2008, 07:13 PM	Tuesday, 2 December 2008, 07:25 PM	Update	40.00

However, for one thing, I need to chase up Tom Cat as he hasn't posted his suggestion yet! Mickey's grade is located along with the first part of my comments. He'll get an email telling him to go and check his score. If I change my mind after I've marked others, I can always click on **Update**, and alter the student's grade.

More than one teacher or class can work on the same assignment in Moodle and have them displayed separately. However, to implement this, you'll have to ask your Moodle administrator to set up groups for you. This isn't something we're looking at right now, but as you get more into Moodle, you'll find it a useful feature.

Other ways to set and mark work in Moodle

If you just want your students to perform a piece of writing, such as an advert, a letter, or a description, then the **Online text** assignment would be the best choice. But there might be times when the students need to actually upload files, such as presentations or leaflets that they have created. Moodle has four types of assignments you can use (although one of them is a bit of a cheat, really). The following table explains the benefits of each one, so that you can select the one that is most suited to your purposes:

Type of assignment	What it's for	Why use it
Online text	Allows students to type straight into Moodle, and allows teachers to correct online	For shorter passages of plain text it's the quickest and simplest way to set and mark work
Upload a single file	Gives students the ability to upload a file, such as a Word-processed document or PowerPoint	For tasks that aren't suited to the online text type, say when you need to upload a certain file type such as a spreadsheet or slideshow
Advanced uploading of files	Students can send more than one item; teachers can return the corrected work for students to revise	If you like commenting on the students' work, but online text isn't for you, you can use this option to mark and return a Word-processed document; you can also use it if you are doing a project involving several pieces of work
Offline text	Students produce work offline, such as a class role play, and it is marked in Moodle	This is just a space in Moodle's grade book for you to record the marks for tasks done outside of Moodle

Have a go hero-mark their campsite design

It's now your turn! The students have uploaded the campsite designs to a database so that everyone can see them. Unfortunately, the designs are not linked to the grade book. However, you could still mark each individual student by using the **Offline text** facility. Why not set it up and see how the grade book appears, ready for you to mark the designs?

Collaborative story-telling

The project is nearly over, but as an entertaining plenary, let's get the students to put their minds and imaginations together to devise a spooky tale about a night on the campsite! We'll help to start them off, and then they can all join in by adding, editing (and even deleting) others' contributions. We shall use a Moodle **wiki** for this, as a wiki is a great tool for collaboration. However, like the glossary, and even the database, a wiki has many more features than we require at present. So we'll just stick to what we need.

Time for action-getting our class to work together on an online story

Let's make things more interesting! Let's ask the students to post an imaginative story.

1. With editing turned on, select the **Wiki** option within the **Add an activity** option.

2. In the **Name** field, provide a suitable title for your wiki, and in the **Description** field, enter a short explanation of what you want the students to add.

3. For the **Type** option, choose **Groups** (we'll take a closer look at the other options, later).

4. Don't worry about the settings that you don't understand. For now, just click on **Save and Display**.

5. On the screen that is displayed next, enter the beginning of the story (or anything you want them to continue with).

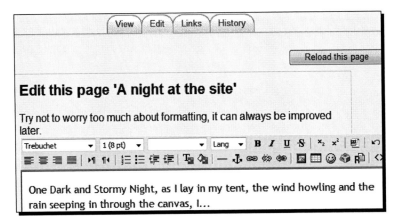

You can add extra pages to a wiki by adding square brackets around the name of the page. The next time that you save it, it will link to the new page. We're just going to have our story on one page, for the sake of simplicity.

What just happened?

The students now have, thanks to our efforts, a communal space on Moodle where they can continue the story. They can click on the **wiki**, enter the desired text into it, and save it, as they would do, if it were a **Forum** or an **Online text** assignment.

The benefit of our group wiki is that our entire class can come to the same page and add, edit, and delete what has been entered. However, if we object to any student's act, we can click on **History** and see who did it, when they did it, and precisely what they did.

Although, we chose **Groups** for our wiki, there are also **Student** and **Teacher** wikis available. The following table provides a very brief outline of the three types of wikis and their uses.

Type of wiki	What it is	Why use it
Groups	One wiki that everyone can edit	Collaborating on a story or group activity
Teacher	Only the teacher can edit this	For presenting information that you can easily add to or edit yourself
Student	Each student has his or her own wiki	As an online exercise book for notes/revisions; private communication between student and teacher

Summary

In this chapter, we used Moodle activities to help us deliver a class project. The added benefit was that we could focus on getting our students to take control of their learning by:

- Getting them to think and reflect on their work in a safe and a moderated environment (using **Forum** and **Chat**)
- Having them share ideas in a **Glossary** and present designs in a **Database**
- Giving them a chance to peer assess, and offering them the opportunity to evaluate their progress privately (using **Choice**)
- Providing online space for them to perform a written task (using an **assignment**)
- Encouraging them to pool ideas and collaborate on a class story (using a **wiki**)

Perhaps, now that we've got them engaged to Moodle, it is time to get some grades in our grade book. The next chapter will teach us to set up interesting exercises for our class students. These exercises will not only be enjoyable for them, but will involve **no marking at all** on our part. Moodle will do it all for us. Interested? Read on!

4
Self-marking Quizzes

This chapter is all about work-life balance. This chapter will teach you how to introduce, practice, and consolidate learning in Moodle through the use of online activities such as quizzes, crosswords, and matching exercises. It will show you how, with the click of a button, you can have differentiated exercises for students of varying abilities. Even better, once you've created it, you can go and have a coffee in the staffroom while Moodle grades it for you and gives your students an instant feedback, which they always appreciate!

For the purposes of this chapter, we're going to assume that the class has been learning about the major world rivers. Thus, we shall:

◆ Test their knowledge with matching, gap-fill, crossword , multi-choice, and jumbled up exercises **that you don't have to mark**

◆ Set an end-of-unit assessment test on Moodle that—once again— **you don't have to mark**

Forget the paper

In the past, we've been used to testing students' knowledge on paper and trying to find ways to make our worksheets a little more appealing than the usual question and answer format. I have spent many hours devising word searches and crosswords in MS Word—or making two columns with pairs of terms for my class to draw lines and to match up the correct pairs. You can do this, unless you want to kill time by getting the students to copy out all of the words in the columns, or draw the crosswords in their exercise books. However, the sheets are of no use once they've been written on. So forget the paper!

Hot potatoes—cool learning

Moodle can make quizzes and matching exercises as mentioned above, with the added bonus that you don't have to mark them. We'll look at Moodle's offerings later in this chapter. However, there's another program available on the Internet that will enable you to do this kind of activity in double-quick time. It has a very bizarre name, which is, **Hot Potatoes**. It's not a part of Moodle but it can be used in Moodle in a very simple and effective manner. Many teachers actually prefer it to the homegrown Moodle version. It has five types of activities that can be created while staying offline on your computer, and uploaded later to Moodle. Moreover, subject to certain conditions, you don't have to pay a single penny. So let's go and get it now!

Hot Potatoes is free for download and use if you are in an educational institution, and your exercises are available freely on the Web. However, if your school wants to put the Hot Potatoes exercises onto a password-protected Moodle site, then it does need to apply for a license to do so. This will cost money. As a teacher, you need not worry about that, unless you are the Moodle Admin of your school. But the link to find out more is here: `http://www.halfbakedsoftware.com/hot_pot_licence.php`.

Time for action-getting a program to create our self-marking activities

Let's download a program that will self-mark various activities in Moodle. Hot Potatoes is one such famous program.

1. Go to the web address, `http://hotpot.uvic.ca/#downloads`.
2. For PC users, click on the top link and then choose **Run**, as shown in the following screenshot:

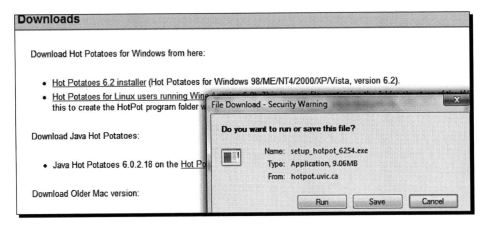

3. If you get any security warnings, agree to them and allow the setup to run (it's quite safe!). Click on **Next** to continue with the set up.

4. Select your language.

5. Accept the license agreement (as mentioned above) and click on **Next** until the software has been installed.

6. When an image of a hand holding a potato appears, click on that image to bring up the following screen:

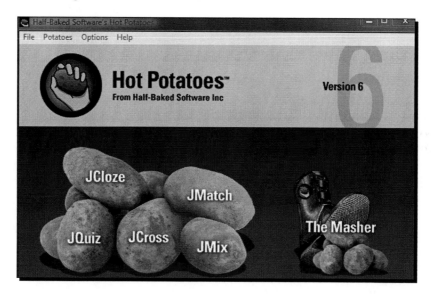

7. Click on **Help** and then click on **Register** (you first need to register—for free—to make full use of the exercises).

8. Click on **Get a key**.

9. Follow the instructions on the site, to get your key emailed to you.

10. Check your email and enter the key along with your username, as shown in the preceding screenshot.

11. You're ready to go.

What just happened?

We have downloaded the Hot Potatoes program—which will enable us to make some self-marking exercises for our Moodle course—to our home computer. We had to register ourselves first to get started with the program but, there's nothing confidential about an email address, so it's quite safe to submit it.

Why not get your school technical support person to put it on your school's computers as well?

Each potato hides a different activity. We aren't bothered about **The Masher**. This helps you link Hot Potatoes together, but you have to pay for it. Thus, we don't need it. Once you've created a couple of activities, you'll get accustomed to the way they work, and you'll be creating them in no time at all. In fact, you can have a match up exercise created, uploaded, and ready for your students to use in less than ten minutes when you know how to do it. We're going to develop a lesson about famous rivers, on Moodle, using all five Hot Potatoes exercises. Here is a simple table that shows what they all do:

Name	What it does	Do we need it?
JMatch	Makes matching drag and drops	YES—it is simple and effective
JCross	Makes crosswords (including ones with images or sound)	YES—it has got a lot of potential
JCloze	Makes gap-fills of varying levels of difficulty	YES—It can be made as easy or as hard as you like
JQuiz	Makes multiple choice exercises	YES—It is simpler than the Moodle equivalent
JMix	Makes jumbled sentences	YES—It is a bit like magnetic fridge poetry
The Masher	Creates sequences of exercises that have been already made	NO—has to be bought and is not really essential for us

Time for action-matching rivers to continents with the JMatch Hot Potato

I'm going to get my students to match up the five rivers with the continents they're situated in. I'm going to set a time limit on it: really quick—maybe a minute. Later, we'll do all of this together in lesson time,as I have a projector. I'll upload it to Moodle so that, for homework, they can each try to beat the time we got in class. Here goes:

1. Click on **JMatch**. When the box comes up, type in a title and put your pairs in (correctly matched up) order, as shown in the following screenshot:

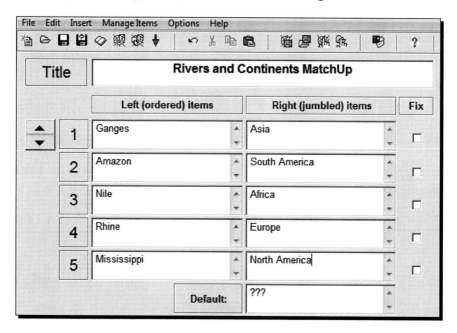

2. If you want more than five pairs, click the arrow next to **1**.

3. Once you have specified all of the pairs that you want to use, click on **File** and then click on **Save**. And you are done!

 That's as easy as it can be. However, you will get a rather blank and grey looking matching exercise that will not inspire your students, visually, to give it a go. Let's try to pretty it up a bit first, before we save it and upload it into Moodle.

4. On the top menu bar, click on **Options** and then **Configure output**, to display the screen shown in the following screenshot:

5. Click on each tab and personalise your activity according to the following table:

Item	What it is	What I think
Title/Instructions	Change the default subtitle and instructions here.	Useful if you want to make the exercise simpler for younger students
Prompts/feedback	Choose how you'll respond to right/wrong answers, and how you'll tell them their score.	Another way that you can personalize your activity*
Buttons	More options to personalize the wording of the activity.	Important: Deselect the **'next exercise'** and **'go to '** buttons.
Appearance	Change the color of the page and text, here.	Click on the rainbow to select a color. This will be previewed on the screen, to the left. Do think of color-blind and dyslexic students, though!
Timer	Set a time limit here and there will be a clock ticking away.	Select the **'set a time limit'** box; then you can choose seconds and/or minutes.
Other	Change the order of the items every time someone opens the activity here (if you want).	I never bother with this myself.
Custom	Options for editing the code behind the activity.	Don't even look at this bit.
CGI	Lets people without Moodle send results via email.	You don't need this!

6. When you are satisfied, click on **OK** at the bottom of the configuration screen to get back to your matching exercise.

Let's have a quick look at **Buttons**. The Hot Potatoes program assumes that you're going to make a series of exercises. Thus, the Hot Potatoes program links them and automatically inserts a link on its page, which will lead you to the next exercise. However, as we are only going to be uploading one exercise at a time, we need to get rid of that link. Otherwise, the children—ever curious—will click on it and find that they reach a Page Not Found and may get confused. That's why it is important to deselect the two options mentioned in the preceding table.

7. Go to **File**, click **Save as**, and give your matchup exercise a name.

What just happened?

We created and saved our first matching exercise using the Hot Potatoes **JMatch** option. We changed the color of the page, added a timer (30 seconds in this case), and abolished the confusing link buttons and non-existent exercises. The exercise is now ready to be uploaded into Moodle, but we need to test it out! Let's have a look at the preview of our matching activity!

To see what it will look like on Moodle, we have to view it as a web page. To do that, we click on **File** and then on **Create Web Page**, as shown in the following screenshot:

JMatch has three different formats. I've listed and explained them in the following table:

Format	What it is	What I think
Flash card	Shows one pair; student guesses the match and then clicks to see if he or she is right	Useful for very young children to introduce/ consolidate knowledge, but older students find it very boring
Standard	Gives one pair and a drop-down menu to choose the match from	Quite simple to see but not very exciting
Drag/Drop	You drag the half on the right onto its matching pair on the left	Best for using with a projector and most popular with students too, especially when timed.

Have a go hero-make the rivers and continents into a drag-and-drop activity

Here's a small activity for you. Prepare a drag-and-drop activity for the rivers and continents.

1. Go to **File** and then click on **Create Web Page**.
2. Choose **Drag/drop** and save it, after giving it an appropriate name.

3. Choose the option: **View the Exercise in my browser**.

4. Try it!

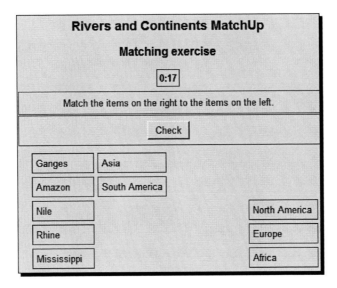

Students like colorful backgrounds added to their activities, but you have to careful that you don't go over the top with gaudy combinations! The rivers and continents matchup is actually blue on yellow; one of the color schemes I understand is easily viewable by dyslexic children. You drag the continent (on the righthand side) over to the river (on the lefthand side) to match them. Can you see the timer at the top of the screen? Once done, you need to click on **Check** to get your score.

Let's have a quick word about **Names**. Did you notice the first time we saved this activity by going to **File** and then clicking on **Save as**, its name (or filename) ended in `.jmt`? The second time it was saved, as a web page, it ended up in `.html`. It doesn't matter to Moodle which one you upload and use, but if you want to alter the exercise, you need to make sure that you have the first version saved. It should be saved as it is in the project file, or else, the draft version might get edited. The other Hot Potato project files end in a similar way according to which one you are using—`.jcl`, `.jcw`, `.jqz` and `.jmx`.

Okay, so we have created our matching activity. Remember that we had actually put the pairs in the correct order to start with? When it goes on Moodle for our class to do, Moodle will mark it according to what we set up—so with that initial first effort, our marking is now at an end! Just one more step and that is—getting it up there for the children to try.

Time for action-getting our matching activity into Moodle

We have created the matching activity on our computer. It's now time to have it uploaded into Moodle.

1. With editing turned on, select **Add an Activity** and then select Hot Potatoes **Quiz**.

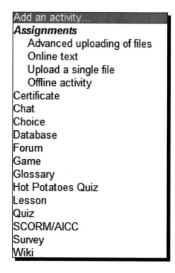

2. In the **Name** block, choose **Specific text** and type in a suitable name for the children to see and click on.

3. Click on **Choose or Upload a file**.

4. Browse your computer and upload the file, as we did for other resources (you can use the .jmt or the HTML version)

5. Ignore anything that you're not sure about as it is—it's safer!

6. In the **Grades** option, if you wish, choose the maximum mark that you want to score the students out of.

7. In the **Grading method** drop-down window, if you wish, decide which mark to choose if they have several attempts.

8. Click on **Save** and return to course.

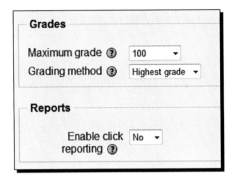

What just happened?

Our Hot Potatoes matching exercise is now in Moodle, and ready to be tried out! We uploaded it similar to how we uploaded other resources such as Word-processed documents. However, we had to upload it into a specific part of Moodle—the Hot Potatoes **Quiz** area. Although this part of Hot Potatoes says "quiz", this is the upload area for all five types of Hot Potatoes activities. If you can't see the Hot Potatoes **Quiz** option when you select **Add an activity...**, then you need to ask your Moodle Admin to **unhide** it—which means that they need to open its eye in the site admin on the front page. We need to load it in this way for it to work in Moodle's grade book. If we'd just added our exercises in **Add a resource...** | **Link to a file or web site**, it would still work, but the marks wouldn't be saved.

Consolidating knowledge with Hot Potatoes activities

Once you've worked one of the Hot Potato applications, you'll get the hang of the configuration screen and the process of uploading the exercise into Moodle. The other exercise types are fairly similar. It'd be quite nice to provide a selection for the students. However, in my experience, there's nothing wrong with using the same vocabulary or questions in each exercise. The students get to practice their learning in five different ways. Thus, by the end, they will identify with it—inside out and upside down! Let's re-jig our rivers and continents exercise in four new ways. The instructions don't need to be quite as detailed, now that we've got one under our belt.

Time for action-creating a self-marking gap-fill exercise

Let's re-equip the Rivers and Continents exercise and create a self-marking, gap-fill exercise:

1. Click on the **JCloze** Potato.

2. Give your gap-fill exercise a name by entering it in the **Title** box. In the window that pops up, type (or copy and paste) the passage in which you want to have gaps.

3. Select a word that you want blanked out, and click on **Gap** at the bottom of the screen.

4. If you wanted, you could add a clue and alternative correct answers for the gapped word, as shown in the following screenshot:

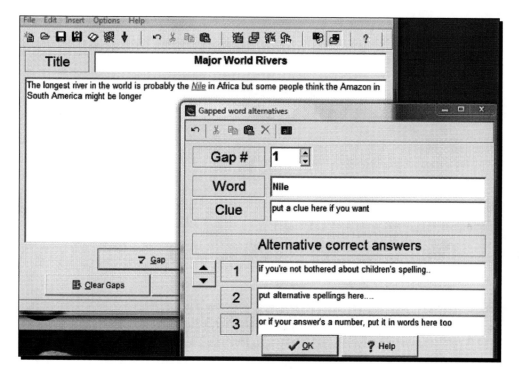

5. Click on **OK** to go back to the main screen.

6. Repeat this for as many blanks or gaps as you want.

7. Go to the configuration screen and personalize your exercise, as we did for the **JMatch** exercise.

8. Click on the **Other** tab, and, with the help of the following table, make your choices specific to **JCloze**:

Item	What it is	What I think
Include SCORM 1.2 functions	One way of including images, sound, or video.	We're not going to use this.
Use a drop down list instead of a text box	Students don't type in their answers; they choose them from a list.	Use this if your children's literacy skills are not good enough that they can type the answers by themselves.
Include word list with text	The missing words are shown along the top of the exercise.	You could do this and then get your students to copy and type the answers into the box.
Make answer checking case sensitive	Students will get it wrong if they use (for example) lower case instead of upper case.	Depends on whether you're testing punctuation or knowledge; I don't use it myself at this level – but I am not an English teacher.
Include a key pad to help the students type non-Roman characters	This brings up foreign language diacritics that they can click on to select them.	If it is a foreign language task and you are testing spelling, use it; if not—don't!

9. Save your gap-fill in a way similar to how you had saved your **JMatch**. Choose **Create Web page** if you want to view and test it.

What just happened?

In double-quick time (I hope!) we used the **JCloze** Hot Potato to make a gap-fill, or cloze, exercise where our students have to fill in the correct rivers to go with the relevant continents. We have personalized its color and wording, perhaps added a timer, and are just about ready to upload it into Moodle.

Have a go hero-make differentiated exercises for students with mixed abilities

You must have noticed in the preceding table that the **Other** section provides you with two options to choose from. The first option will give a list of the missing words at the top of your gap-fill and the second option will offer a drop-down box for less confident spellers. Why not go and make two **JCloze** exercises? One JCloze exercise can be created for the students to have a guess and type in the names of the rivers or continents themselves with no help at all. Another JCloze exercise can be created where the students are provided with either the words to be copied by them, or a drop-down list. Alternatively, you could set a longer time limit for students with a lower ability, or allow them as much time as they need.

Time for action-making a self-marking crossword exercise

This one's probably my favorite. Don't be put off by it! As soon as you open it, it looks complex, but I have a method for creating the crosswords in double-quick time. Thus, let us just follow these instructions and then go and watch some TV. Crosswords are popular with some students, but not all children actually know how to fill them in. Also, the Hot Potatoes crosswords don't operate in the way you expect them to, so you might need to explain a bit about it to the students. Let's learn how to do it.

1. Click on **JCross**.

2. Type in the title of your crossword, in the box on the left.

3. Click on **Manage Grid**, which is available on the top menu.

4. Add the words that you want in your crossword, one under the other, as shown in the following screenshot:

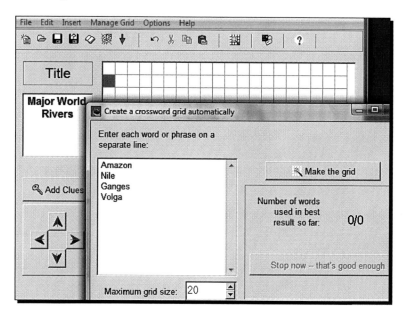

5. Click on the **Make the grid** button.

6. When you're happy with the results and are back on the main screen, click on **Add Clues**.

7. Select the word that you want to give a clue for. Type the clue in the box and click on **OK**, as shown in the following screenshot:

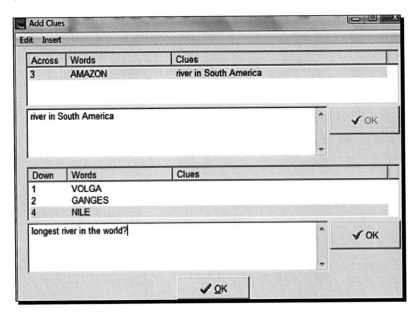

8. Click on the **OK** button—with the green tick mark—at the bottom of the screen, when you are done with adding the clues.

9. Go to the configuration screen to personalize your crossword.

10. In the **Other** tab, select **Show All clues below the crossword grid**.

11. Save your crossword, in a similar way, as you saved the **JMatch** and **JCloze** exercises. Use the option, **Create Web page**, if you want to preview and test it.

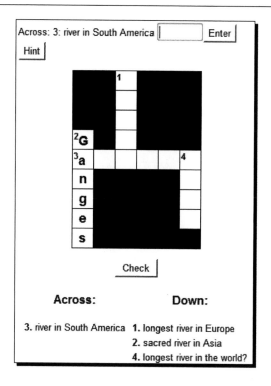

What just happened?

We used the **JCross** Hot Potato application to create a crossword, which our students can fill in online. They'll be graded by Moodle, instead of by us. We have personalized the colors, made sure that the clues were listed under the crossword, and even set a timer. This exercise can be uploaded to Moodle in exactly the same way as the other Hot Potatoes applications.

Let's have a word about the crossword application. The Hot Potato crossword doesn't show the clues by default—that's the reason why, we made sure that we included them when we configured the display. Nor do you type your answers into the boxes—you type your answers by clicking on a clue number and then entering the word in the box that comes up. Try it—you'll need to explain this to your students before they attempt to solve a crossword.

Time for action-making a self-marking mixed up words exercise

Another application of Hot Potatoes is called **JMix**. This is helpful for creating activities where the students have to rearrange words or phrases. If you save it as a web page (`.html`), you can set it up in two different ways. You can either set it up in such a way that when the students click on the word or the phrase, it magically moves itself into the next part of a sentence, or you can have it as a drag-and-drop activity. We're going to set up our application to put the correct rivers in the correct continents—again! This information will be indelibly printed on their brains once they've been through every Hot Potato! Let's learn how to set it up.

1. Click on **JMix**.

2. Enter a name in the **Title** box.

3. In the **Main sentence** box, type in your sentences—a few words at a time, separating them one under the other, as shown in the following screenshot:

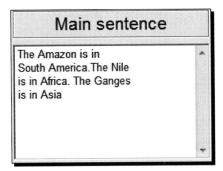

4. Think about possible alternate correct answers and add them to **Alternate Sentences**.

 Alternate Sentences means that there is another way that the answer could be read, and still be right. For instance, if I did **London/is/the capital of/England**, then it could work equally correct as **the capital of England is London** (if we disregard case)   Thus, we need to enter that sentence as well, so that the children aren't penalized for a different turn of phrase.

5. Go to the configuration screen and personalize your exercise.

6. Save the exercise, in a similar way, as we saved the **JMatch**, the **JCross** and the **JCloze** exercises.

7. Use the **Create Web Page** option to view this exercise in two different styles.

What just happened?

We made use of the **JMix** application of Hot Potatoes, to create a scrambled up exercise where students will have to reorder parts of a sentence or sentences to make a meaningful passage. We shall upload it into Moodle in the same way as we loaded the other Hot Potatoes applications, although we have two ways of displaying it as an .html file. Which one do you prefer?

The standard format appears as shown in the following screenshot:

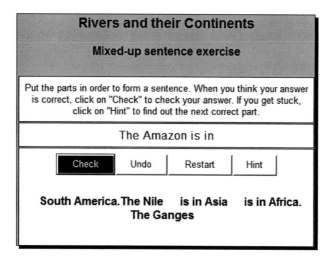

In the standard format, each time the students click on a word or phrase, it is attached to the previous phrase they clicked on. The drag-and-drop format looks like this:

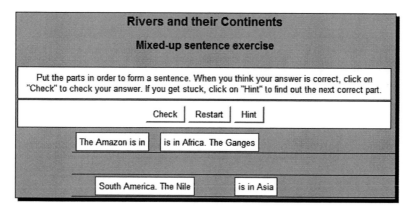

Your choice might depend on your personal experience with the students. Being a teacher, you'd know more about their preferences.

Time for action-making a self-marking multiple-choice quiz

There's a lot of 'Action' in this chapter! But it should get easier and quicker with each attempt. We're going to ask questions about rivers and the continents they're in, and give our students a choice of answers. You can make multiple choice quizzes in Moodle (and we shall), but Hot Potatoes are much simpler!

The first time that you click on the **JQuiz** potato, you'll be asked the question— **Beginner or Advanced?** This is to enquire whether you want to start in the **beginner** or in the **advanced** mode. The main difference between the two is that, with advanced mode, you can award percentages of marks to each alternative answer, unlike in the beginner mode—where only one answer is 100% correct, and the others are totally wrong.

1. Click on **JQuiz**.

2. In the **Title** box, enter a name for your exercise.

3. Type in your first question in the box next to **Q1**.

4. Type in the possible answers in the boxes next to **A, B, C**, and so on below **Answers**.

5. If you wanted to, you could add **Feedback** for each answer.

6. Select the checkbox for the correct answer, below the **Settings** button.

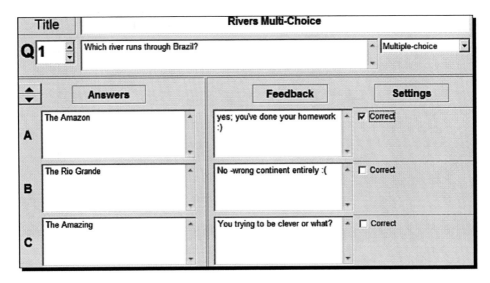

7. Click the arrows to the left of the **Answers** block to add another question.

8. Repeat the process until you're done adding all of your questions.

9. Go to the configuration screen to personalize your multi-choice exercise.

10. Save the exercise in the same way as you did for the other Hot Potatoes exercise, choosing **Create Web page** to preview and test your exercise.

What just happened?

We used the **JQuiz** Potato to make a multiple-choice exercise to test our students' knowledge of rivers and continents. We have personalized the application's text and colors, and maybe added a timer, and are now ready to upload it into Moodle—just as we did the others.

 If you click on the drop-down menu and select the option **Multiple-Choice**, to the top right of the screen (as shown in the preceding screenshot), you'll see that there are actually other types of question that we could have used.

Here's a table to explain what the drop-down menu options do, and why you might want to use them:

Type of question:	What it is	Why use it
Short answer	Students type an answer into a text box.	Offers more scope, but you need to think of all possible permutations, or else, the students might find it tough to solve.
Hybrid	If they can't type in the correct answer after a certain number of tries, they get the question as a multiple-choice instead.	This might be useful if you think the students might have problems with your short answer questions. But if you think that way, why not just go for the multi-choice in the first place?
Multi-select	Students can choose more than one correct answer.	Useful if you want them to select a group of items—such as 'Which of the following rivers are in Europe'?

Adding pictures to our Hot Potatoes

If you search the Internet, you'll find all types of fancy Hot Potatoes exercises including sound files, photos, and even video clips or animations. You could devote a whole book to Hot Potatoes. However, right now, we don't have the time to study any more of its complexities.

Images can be used very effectively, and are not very difficult to add, either. Let's finish off our journey into the Hot Potatoes country by looking at a **JMatch** exercise, where instead of matching the rivers with the continents, our pupils need to actually recognize the outline of the continents.

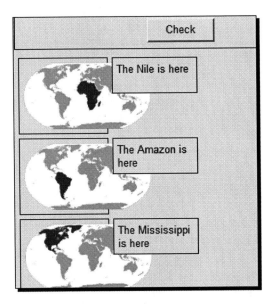

Time for action-creating an exercise where words are matched with pictures

Let's create an exercise, using **JMatch**, where our pupils need to recognise the outline of the continents.

1. Have your images (not very large in size) saved on your computer and ready for use (we shall learn more about image sizes and types in Chapter 8).

2. Click on **JMatch**.

3. As with our first **JMatch**, give the exercise a name and add the words, "half of the pair".

4. Save the exercise as a project file (`.jmt`).

5. Go to a box in which you want to insert the image, and click inside it.

6. From the menu at the top of the screen, select **Insert | Picture | Picture from Local File**, as shown in the following screenshot:

7. Browse for an image of your choice, as you'd do while finding one for a Moodle exercise.

8. In the next dialog box (**Picture alignment**), ignore it for now and click on **OK**.

9. You will be taken back to the main screen, and your chosen box or boxes will have web code in it, as shown in the following screenshot. That's fine; don't worry!

10. Go to the configuration screen to personalize your exercise.

11. Select menu option **File** at the top of the screen, and then select **Create zip package**.

12. If you want to preview or test your exercise, choose **Create Web page**.

What just happened?

We created another matching exercise. However, this time—because we added images—we had to save it in a slightly different way. This is because Moodle needs to have the uploaded images as well as the matchup file for the images, in order for them to work together online. We saved everything together as a zipped (or compressed) folder. We shall need to upload that zipped folder into Moodle and unzip it, before getting our Hot Potatoes picture matchup exercise ready for our students. This is where you come in!

Have a go hero-put a Hot Potato exercise with pictures onto Moodle

You may remember that, in Chapter 2, we zipped an entire folder of slideshows rather than loading them one at a time—we are going to do pretty much the same thing, here.

1. Click on the **Files** option in the Moodle course admin block.

2. Upload the zipped Hot Potatoes package that we have created.

3. Unzip the folder.

4. Select menu option **Add an Activity | Hot Potatoes | Quiz**.

5. When prompted to choose a file, choose the `.html` file from the unzipped package.

6. Save it, and check whether that works.

Words of warning

There are two points to be made here—not to put you off Hot Potatoes, but just to make you aware.

Hot Potatoes quizzes are great fun and very useful as home work, consolidating what's been taught in class. However, they shouldn't really be used as assessment tests—crafty children, over the years, have found ways to get the answers without thinking too hard. They'll press the back button for instance, if they get one wrong, and allow themselves another try. Some of my students also have discovered that if you click on **Hint**, you get one letter of the word. When the **Hint** button is pressed again, you get another letter—until you get the whole word given to you. If you want to set a test in Moodle that you don't have to mark (and who wouldn't?) and is pretty much hack-proof, then you should use the **Moodle quiz**—as we shall be doing next.

Making an assessment test with a Moodle quiz

The name **quiz** is a bit of a misnomer really, as it makes me think of TV game shows. To Moodle, a quiz is just a module where you can add different types of questions for your students, which is not, usually, as exciting as it sounds (if you want excitement, read the next chapter on games!). What we're going to do, is test our students' knowledge of the World's rivers in a timed assessment. Moodle's quiz isn't currently as friendly as Hot Potatoes, but I'm using it because it's **safer** for an exam.

Time for action-set up a Moodle quiz as test on rivers and continents

Let's create a quiz to test our students' knowledge about the World's rivers in a timed assessment.

1. In the **Name** block, type a name for your quiz that the pupils will see, and click on.

2. In the **Description** block, enter a description of the quiz.

3. Select your options for the quiz in the boxes that follow—if in doubt, leave them the way they are; it's quite safe!

4. Use the following table to help you make your choices (for our test, we need to set the timer as well as a password).

Item	What it is	What I think
Timing	Set start, end, and length of test—we've seen this before.	Select **Enable time limit** for them to see a clock as they work.
Display	How it will look on the page.	Keep it at **Unlimited**. The students then scroll down to see all the questions.
Attempts	How many attempts they get, and if they will be penalized for extra attempts.	For tests, set it to **1** attempt. Set **Adaptive mode** to **No** and don't even bother to look at what it means.
Grades	For a test, keep it at the highest grade.	Make sure **Penalties** is set to **No**.
Review options	When they get feedback and what feedback they get.	So many choices here—click the **?** for help, or leave it as it is.
Security	For setting a password.	Type in a password next to **Require password**—tell your class on the day. You can change it, for another class, another day.
Common module settings	For groups in the grade book.	Ignore unless your administrator has set you up with groups.
Overall feedback	Sets a comment at the end, according to how the students did.	A nice touch but you must fill in every box—see the following screenshot.

In the overall feedback form, fill in your feedback—with respect to the marks the student scores. An example is shown in the following screenshot:

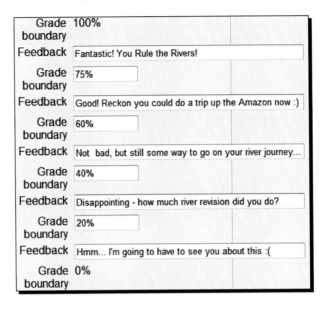

5. Click on **Save and display**.

6. You'll get the quiz question on the screen, in two parts, as shown in the following screenshot:

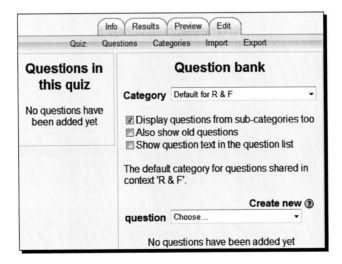

What just happened?

We've set up the front page of the Moodle quiz that will be our assessment test. We've decided on how the quiz will be presented to the students, and what feedback they will get. If you look on your course page, you'll see it there—but, it's an empty exercise. We haven't actually added any questions to it yet. See what I meant about Hot Potatoes quizzes being friendlier?

The quiz question screen is in two parts

The left side of the screen is where your questions will be displayed once you've created them. On the right is the storage area for the questions. If you want to organize your quiz questions into categories, you can do that. However, we don't want any extra steps so, as beginners, we'll use the default. There are many different types of questions. However, some are easier when compared to others. Let's try the three easiest ones and then look briefly at the other possibilities later.

Time for action-making a multiple-choice question

Let's create a multiple-choice question in Moodle.

1. Click under **Create new**, and choose **Multiple-choice**.

2. In the **Name** block, give the question a name—not Question 1 (you put all of your questions for all your quizzes into here, so you need a more descriptive name for the question).

3. In the **Question text** block, type in the actual question.

4. In the **Choice** sections, enter the alternative answers (with feedback, if you opted for it).

5. For the correct answer, change the **Grade** to **100%**, by selecting this from the drop-down menu.

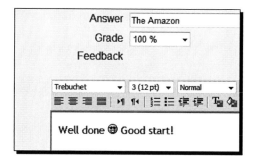

6. Save the question.

7. In the question bank, click on the arrow next to your question to move it over to the lefthand side—the quiz area—as shown in the following screenshot:

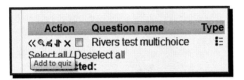

Time for action-making a true/false question

Let's create an exercise in Moodle, consisting of questions that are to be answered with a **True** or a **False**.

1. Click on **Create new** and choose the option **True/False**.

2. In the **Question name** block, give your question a descriptive name (not number!).

3. In the **Question text** block, type in your question. A true or false exercise on Rivers and Continents will appear as shown in the following screenshot.

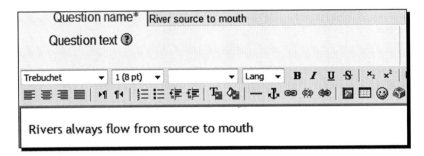

4. In the **Correct answer**, decide if the statement is **True** or **False,** and indicate this accordingly.

5. Add **Feedback**, if you have opted for it.

6. Save the question.

7. Add it to the left-hand side of the quiz area.

Time for action-making a matching question

Let's create an exercise—based on a matching question—on Moodle.

1. Click on **Create new**, and choose **Matching**.

2. In the **Question name** block, give your question a descriptive name (not number!).

3. In the **Question text** block, explain what they have to match up.

4. For each question, type a simple question in the **Question** block, and in the **Answer** field, type the answer. You need a minimum of three question/answer pairs for the matches to work. It doesn't have to be a proper question or answer—check out the one on rivers, here:

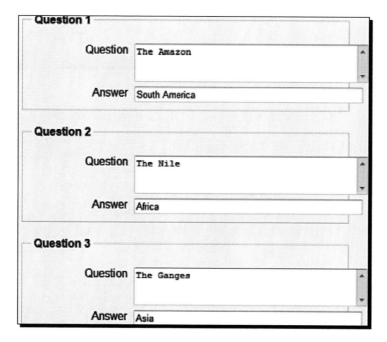

5. Save the question.

6. Add it to the quiz area, in a way similar to how you did for the previous two exercises.

What just happened?

We now (at last!) have a Moodle quiz, with three different types of questions. We had to set it up first, and then add the questions, one by one, choosing the type we wanted. The questions can be used again and may be accessed by any teacher in that course.

To re-order the questions, we just click on the up and down arrows on the left side of the quiz area. To preview the quiz and check whether it works click on the **Preview** tab at the top. You can see both of the options in the following screenshot:

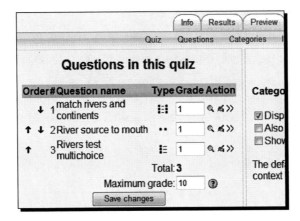

Moodle has been saving these questions to our course page as we've gone along. If you're interested, let's see how our—three rivers—questions will appear to our students (I've answered them, by the way).

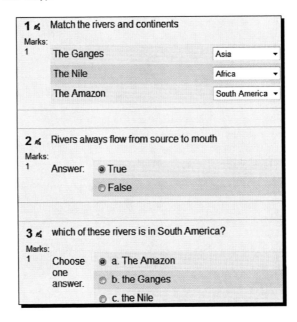

Other types of questions

For our assessment test, we have used the three simplest types of question. At the start, I did say that there were other types of questions that are also a part of the Moodle. The Moodle quiz is very powerful as it has a lot of potential and a variety of questions; but it is also very complex. I've summarized the other question types here. Some of them you might like to try. Others, I really wouldn't recommend, and would suggest that you look at Hot Potatoes instead:

Question type	What it is	What I think
Calculated	Numbers questions with formulae.	Perhaps more suited to older students.
Description	Not a question—just a space for some text.	You can use it as a passage on which you can base your subsequent questions.
Essay	Space for text and your question, and student gets big space for long answer.	You have to mark this yourself—Moodle can't!
Short answer	The student types in a word or phrase, as his/her answer to your question.	You need to be careful to cover all possible permutations!
Numerical	For sums.	Looks like a short answer, but students type numbers instead of words.
Random short answer matching	Matching (as we did) but with answers from the short answer questions.	I haven't found much use for this at our level.
Embedded answer or cloze	Moodle's version of gap-fill.	Needs some knowledge of coding; I find J-Cloze to be quicker to set up.

Summary

In this chapter, we've created a variety of activities to test our students' knowledge of the World's rivers. We've set up all the activities, which are going to mark themselves in Moodle. In this chapter, we:

- Created a matching exercise with words, and also a matching exercise with pictures
- Created a gap-fill exercise, which can be adapted for both high-ability and lower-ability children
- Created a crossword that the students can enjoy solving, either individually on the computer, or in the class—using a projector
- Mixed up some clauses and got the students to think and reorder them correctly
- Created a multiple-choice exercise for homework
- Designed a timed and password protected, end of unit test in Moodle, with three different types of questions

I said at the start, that this chapter was all about work/life balance. After the Work—of setting up my Hot Potatoes exercises and my end of unit assessment—I can now enjoy my Life—sitting back and letting Moodle mark and record the grades for me. And then—in Chapter 5—it's time to play some games!

5
Games

This chapter is all about having fun! Not only do our students enjoy playing games that help them learn, but often, we enjoy watching them play—for everyone it acts as a welcome change from the dry text-book work. The following games are from sites that offer free, or good value, games for educational purposes. Games appeal to younger children because of their animations, sound effects, and (in a couple of cases) rather cruel nature! We're going to enhance our units on river processes and flooding by using some easy-to-set-up games. For one of the games, Moodle can do the grading for us—so while the students are enjoying playing, Moodle is keeping our grade book updated.

In this chapter, we shall:

- ◆ Test our students' knowledge of flooding terminology, with the help of a space-age hangman game.

- ◆ Check the students' understanding of river processes, with the help of a dustbin sorting game.

- ◆ Make the students split mountains from rivers with the help of a great noisy hammer.

- ◆ Give the students a chance to practice their spellings with a fun WordWeb.

- ◆ Assign the students homework—marked for us by Moodle—on the New Orleans flood. For this activity, their reward will be to catapult their Head Teacher (or us, the teachers!) into the sunset.

So let's get on with it.

Making an Alien Abduction (hangman) game

The web site that we're going to use for this game is `http://www.what2learn.com/`. This web site has a number of free games that teachers can create online, and link to from their Moodle site. I've found, as a High School teacher, that my 11-14 year old students are all too keen to look for game web sites when they should be online working on their history homework. They'll actually love being able to play online games with your blessing—but you'll still have control.

Time for action-finding and making the Alien Abduction game

Let's first find and then create a game named Alien Abduction.

1. Go to the web address `http://www.what2learn.com/`.

2. Click on **Make a game** (as shown in the following screenshot).

3. Next, click on **Alien Abduction**. You'll see that there are other games as well—which you can create some other time.

4. Click on the green arrow saying **Make a game**, that comes up next.

5. Start typing in the names of the objects that you want to include in the game. We need to enter a title and eight words. Ours is about flooding; so it might look a bit like the following screenshot:

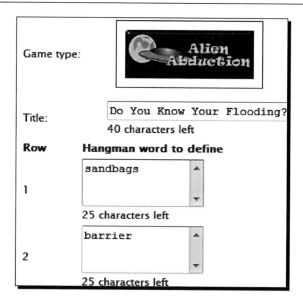

6. Click on **Confirm Questions** at the bottom of the screen. You don't need to add a tag.

7. On the next page, check your words and click on **Create Game**.

8. That's it! Done! You'll get the following message, displaying the number allotted to your game:

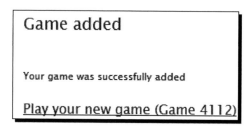

9. If you click on the link **Play your new game** followed by the number allotted to the game, it will take you to your game.

What just happened?

We created a hangman-style game, online, by entering our choice of words and then saving the game on the web site. We've been provided with a link to our game, which students can click on, to play the game.

In this game, as shown in the following screenshot, children have to guess the words before the spaceship comes down and beams up Granny. Be warned—some of your students might deliberately get it wrong just to see what happens! It's only fair to let them do it once; I did, out of curiosity!

Have a go hero-adding a link to a web site in Moodle

Now, we just need to get it into Moodle—which is something that we've already done several times in the previous chapter. Do you remember how?

1. With editing turned on, click on **Add a Resource**
2. Choose the option **Link to a file or website**
3. Type, or copy and paste, the link to the game, into the **Location** box
4. Select the **Open in a new window** option
5. Click on **Save** and return to the course

A quick way to copy and paste a web site address (URL) is to select it with your mouse and then press *Ctrl+C*, on the keyboard, and then go to where you want to paste it and press *Ctrl+V*.

Garbage in the bins—making a sorting exercise

Our next game will get our students to separate the true statements about river processes from the ones that I have invented. The site I am using this time is `http://www.classtools.net`, a site made by teacher Russell Tarr for other teachers to use—for free. This web site has a wide variety of activities that your students would love, but we're going to focus on the bin game. This needs one more step than our previous game did, but it is well worth that extra five minutes. Students enjoy playing the bin game, as they love the sounds made when they get the correct items in the correct bins.

Time for action-finding and making the bin game

Let's find and create a bin game, where the student is expected to decide which statements are true and which are false, by dropping the statements into the correct bin.

1. Go to the web address `http://www.classtools.net`.

2. Click on **Select a Template**, and then choose **Dustbin Game**, as shown in the screenshot below.

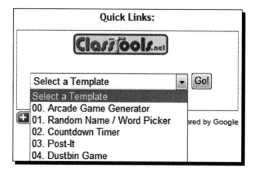

3. Click on **Go!**.

4. When you get to the **How to Play** screen, click on **Start**.

5. Enter your statements in the text boxes (bins) available on the next screen. You'll have four bins; ignore the ones that you don't want to use. Our **True** or **False** sorting exercise, looks like this:

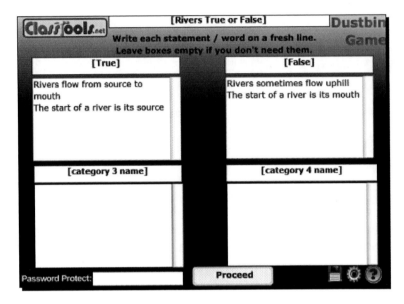

6. Enter a password in the **Password Protect** block, to stop students from being able to alter your words.

7. Click on the blue diskette icon, available to the right of the **Proceed** button.

8. When asked whether you want to open or save the file, choose to save it somewhere on your computer.

9. That's it. Done!

What just happened?

Earlier, we used another web site to create a game that we access on that web site. However, this time, we saved our game as a web page (an .html file like those Hot Potatoes applications in Chapter 4). When we go to Moodle, instead of linking to the web site—where the game is—we actually upload that web page into Moodle.

Have a go hero-adding a link to a file (our game) in Moodle

There's nothing tricky about this part. Upload the game file and the link to the game file in exactly the same way as you uploaded the individual Word-processed documents in Chapter 2. Then play it! As each statement comes up on the screen, you need to drag the statement to the correct bin. Have your sound turned on. See what I meant about the children loving the noise?

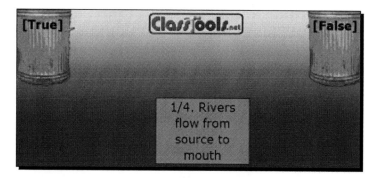

I've used this in languages to get students to separate out masculine and feminine words. I have used the game in English to get the students to distinguish between nouns, verbs, and adjectives. In RE and PSHE, I've seen two bins—statements and opinions. The class must decide which sentences are true and which sentences are not.

Bish Bash Bosh—a differentiation game with a hammer!

The next game also requires the students to pick out words or concepts of a certain type, from a group. But in this game, the students need speed and concentration. The aim of the game is to hit the correct words with a hammer, as they move along the screen. We'll get our younger students to separate mountains from rivers using **Bish Bash Bosh**—one of the several fun activities made by UK teacher, Stewart Davies. It's not like our first two games—where you had to create the game, download it, and then upload it into Moodle. So, once again, we have to put in slightly more effort. Let's take it one step at a time.

Time for action-finding and creating the Bish Bash Bosh game

Let's go online and then create the **Bish Bash Bosh** game.

1. Go to the web address `http://www.sandfields.co.uk/games/`.

2. Scroll down the page until you see the image shown in the following screenshot (which is what the game itself looks like):

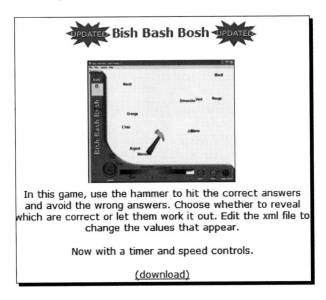

3. Click on the **download** link, and a pop-up window will appear. Click on **Save.**

4. Navigate to the location on your computer where you saved the game. It should be a zipped folder (which has a zipper on its icon).

5. Right-click on this folder and choose **Extract All...** option.

6. Open the newly-extracted folder (which will have same name, but no zipper in the icon!) and you should see the four files shown in the following screenshot:

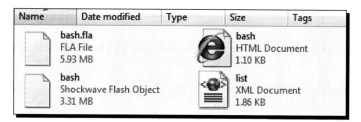

7. Right-click on the file called **List**, and choose **Open With | Notepad** from the context menu.

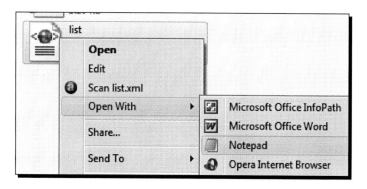

8. Don't panic! You'll see some French words placed in between a lot of punctuation marks (web code, actually). They come in pairs: one word that's `right` (correct) and another one that's `wrong`:

```
list - Notepad
File   Edit   Format   View   Help
<popups>
     <item>
          <right>Rouge</right>
          <wrong>Cinq</wrong>
     </item>
     <item>
          <right>Jauné</right>
          <wrong>Huit</wrong>
     </item>
     <item>
          <right>Bleu</right>
          <wrong>Cent</wrong>
     </item>
```

9. Enter the names of rivers (or names of anything, that you want to be selected) between the `right` HTML tags.

10. Enter the names of mountains (or names of anything, that you want to be avoided) between the `left` HTML tags.

```
list - Notepad

File   Edit   Format   View   Help
<popups>
    <item>
        <right>Thames</right>
        <wrong>Pennines</wrong>
    </item>
    <item>
        <right>Rhine</right>
        <wrong>Alps</wrong>
    </item>
    <item>
        <right>Ganges</right>
        <wrong>Himalayas</wrong>
    </item>
    <item>
        <right>Mississippi</right>
        <wrong>Rockies</wrong>
    </item>
```

11. Overwrite this edited file with the original file, by clicking on **Save**.

12. Right-click on the folder and choose **Rename** (we'll call ours `Bashrivers`).

13. Congratulations! Another game is created!

What just happened?

We went to a web site and downloaded a zipped folder containing a bashing, differentiation game. Once the folder was unzipped, we edited the file called `list.xml` to include the words that we wanted, and then saved it all again but with a new name. If you click on the `.html` file in that new folder, you can actually play the game on your computer. It's hard—you have to chase the river names and bash them with a hammer (great sound effects again), and at the same time you have to avoid the mountains.

Now to get our game into Moodle.

Have a go hero-uploading and displaying our game on Moodle

As you may recall, Moodle won't let you upload folders in the way that they are normally stored on your PC. You have to **zip** or **compress** them first. Then, once you have uploaded them into Moodle's course files, you have to unzip them again. We did this in Chapter 2, with a week's worth of slideshows, if you remember. If you're happy with how to do that, have a go and do it now. However, if you're not, here's a quick recap.

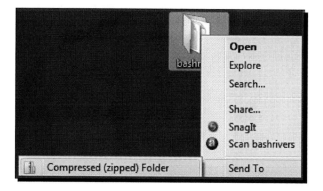

1. Right-click on our game folder and choose **Send To | Compressed (zipped) Folder**.

2. From your Moodle course page, click on **files**, and then upload this zipped folder (the file should have an extension if `.zip`).

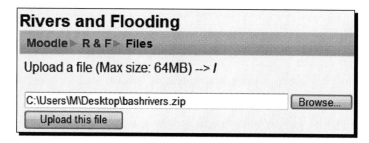

3. Once the file has been uploaded, click on **Unzip**.

4. You'll get a list of the four files inside the zipped file, as shown below. Click the **OK** button at the bottom of the list.

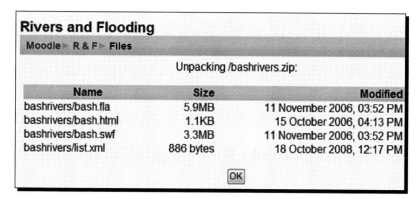

5. You will have a folder with the same name again—but without a `.zip` file extension this time.

6. On your course page, with editing turned on, select **Add a Resource**.

7. Select the option **Link to a file or website,** and then navigate to, and choose, the `.html` file from the folder.

8. Click on **Save and return to course**.

> The file that we altered—did you see it, ending in `.xml`? This is like an information sheet that passes the details onto the rest of the game to make it work. Once you understand that, there are several games that work in the same way—you're about to create another one now.

WordWeb—making a spelling game using Spellmaster

Another source of free games made by a teacher, Frank McAree, is the **Spellmaster** web site on `http://www.spellmaster.com/`. We're going to use one of his games to test our students' spelling. However, we actually get four-in-one here, because we will change a single `.xml` file that is used as an information file by a several different games. We get the chance to play a variety of activities, including a matching game, a concentration game (pelmanism), a word search, and two types of spelling games.

Time for action-finding and making the WordWeb game from Spellmaster

In my opinion, we can whizz through the instructions here, as they're pretty much the same as those for our Hammer game:

1. Go to the web address `http://www.spellmaster.com/`.

2. Click on **Download Pack**, and save and unzip the files, just as we did for **Bish Bash Bosh**.

3. You'll see more files in the folder—no problem! Just find the file named `words`; that's your XML file.

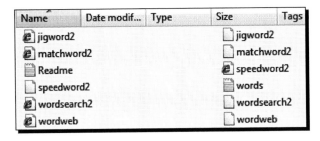

4. Right-click on the file and select **Open With... | Notepad,** as we did earlier.

5. This time, we get a list of French words and their English meanings. Change the pairs of words to whatever you want.

We're matching up rivers and cities, and want our students to be able to locate the rivers correctly, and then spell the main cities that the rivers run through. Our edited file looks like this:

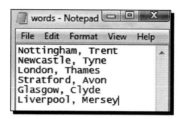

6. Click on **Save**, to save this file and overwrite the original file.

7. Save the entire folder, giving it a new name (we will name ours as `Riverscities`).

What just happened?

We downloaded and unzipped a folder containing a number of games, and also an editable file that we altered to suit our rivers topic. We have renamed the folder and are about to upload it into Moodle.

Have a go hero-uploading and displaying our game in Moodle

Entirely over to you now! The process is the same as before, which is zip, upload, unzip, and then link to one of the HTML files. Let's link to the one called `riverscities/wordweb.html`. We'll get a game that looks like this:

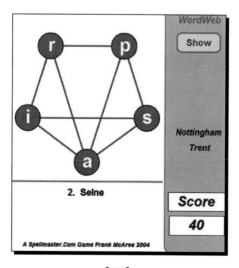

Our students need to think, and work out the main city through which the River Seine runs, and then attempt to spell it correctly—by clicking on the letters in the correct order.

But that's not all! When we edited the `.xml` file (called `words`), it automatically linked itself to the other games in the folder, too. Therefore, if we choose one of the files that has a `.html` extension, this can be played instead, as shown in the matchup activity which we selected by opening the `matchup2` HTML file) in the following screenshot:

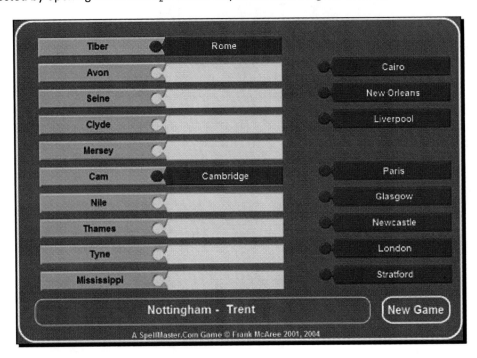

I know what you're thinking!

We're having a lot of fun creating games. We've made two of types of online game and two types of offline game that we've uploaded onto Moodle. Our students will have a lot of fun playing these games, and will appreciate the instant feedback that the activity offers. However, how do we get this past the Head Teacher or parents who see no evidence of what the students have actually achieved? Well, how about making a game that actually **records** their scores in Moodle?

Fling the Teacher—making a Moodle-marked homework

Fling the Teacher is yet another free game created by yet another teacher, Andrew Field (where do these teachers find the time?). Its advantage is that it links to the grade book in Moodle in a way that is not so different from the Hot Potato activities, which we worked on in the previous chapter. So while our youngsters think they're playing a game for homework, you get their results saved in Moodle, to justify their fun!

What's more; I've saved the best until last! In **Alien Abduction**—our first game—the idea was to save Granny from being zapped by the Aliens. The idea here is that our pupils' knowledge won't save their teacher; rather, it will condemn the teacher! It's much more motivating that way! As each question is answered correctly, a trebuchet is constructed, with the head of their teacher on it. Eventually, if all of the questions are answered correctly, the teacher is flung. There is an option at the start to customize the teacher's appearance. I'm not saying that the drawn face will exactly look like that of our Head Teacher. However, I have seen many games played on Moodle with a balding, bespectacled man!

Let's make a game for our eighth year class students (12-13 year olds), who've been studying the flooding in New Orleans, after the Katrina Hurricane occurred. We watched a documentary about the hurricane in our class, and for homework, they were asked to demonstrate how much they could still recollect by playing the game, **Fling the Teacher**.

Time for action-finding and setting up 'Fling the Teacher'

Let's set up the game, **Fling the Teacher**.

1. Go to the web site address `http://www.contentgenerator.net/`.

2. Scroll down and click on the **Free** link, available under the **Fling the Teacher** image, as shown in the following screenshot.

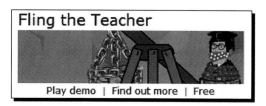

3. Scroll down to **Suite 2: Fling the Teacher**, and click on it.

4. Click on the image that is displayed next, as shown in the following screenshot:

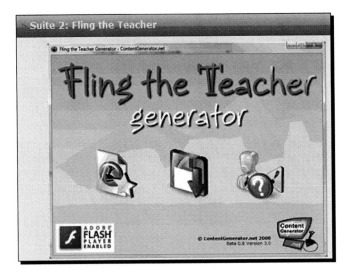

5. When prompted, register on the support forum. Please do so—it's perfectly safe!

6. Scroll down to the bottom of the screen and click on the **Download File** link.

7. A dialog box will be displayed, as shown in the following screenshot. Click on the **Open** button.

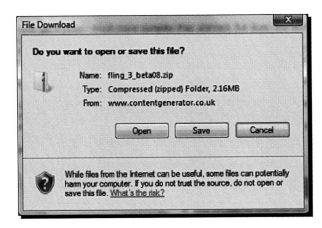

8. When it has opened, click on the **Extract all files** button.

9. You will be warned: "The publisher cannot be verified. Are you sure you want to run this software?" Click **Run**—it's OK—I'll verify him!

10. On Vista, you might be asked if you want to allow this or not. Choose to allow it.

11. When the installation has finished, the game should open up on your computer, and you will get this screen:

12. Click on the icon with the star, located to the left of the screen. (The tooltip text will say **Create a New Game**.)

What just happened?

We just downloaded, unzipped, and opened up another free program that we will use to create a self-marking game. This game will then be uploaded into Moodle and have its scores recorded in the grade book. Let's get back into action straight away, and create the game!

Time for action-creating a 'Fling the Teacher' game

Now, that we have searched and downloaded the **Fling the Teacher** game, let's go ahead and create the game.

1. On the first screen that is displayed when you click on **Create a New Game**, type the title of your new game and your own name (if you want).

2. Click on **Continue**.

3. Type in your question in the _Question_ box, as shown in the following screenshot:

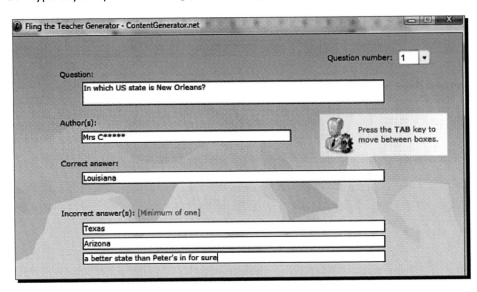

4. Click on the right-pointing arrow at the bottom of the screen to continue.

 Did you see the final incorrect answer that I have entered? We're creating this game for one particular class, and they'll love it if we can personalize it a little—by making references to students in the group or even teachers in the school. I discovered, several years ago, that children are more motivated to persevere with an activity if they think there's a chance they might feature in it somewhere! Keep that in mind as you do the games in this chapter.

5. After a minimum of 15 questions, click on the icon on the far right—**Game setting**.

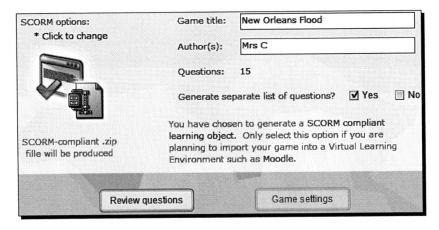

6. We want the **SCORM** option because this will work with our Moodle grade book.

7. Click once more on the **generate game** icon on the far right. You will be prompted for a location to save the file game to, as shown in the following screenshot:

8. You'll be saving the game as a compressed (zipped) folder on your computer.

What just happened?

We have created our game and saved it in as a **SCORM** activity. This is a special type of activity that works in different **Virtual Learning Environments (VLEs)**—such as Moodle—and records the score. Because of this, we need to upload it in a special way for it to work. So, let's do that now:

Time for action-getting our game to work in Moodle's grade book

Now that we have created the game and downloaded it into our computer, let's get the game uploaded into Moodle.

1. With Editing turned on, click on **Add an activity...** option.

2. Choose the option **SCORM/AICC**.

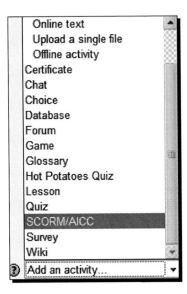

3. You'll get a screen with the options that we've never come across before. Don't panic!

4. Scroll to **Choose or Upload a file**, and upload your `Fling the Teacher` zipped folder (`NewOrleans.zip`) into the course files in the same way as we've done for other zipped folders in this chapter.

5. Do not unzip it! Click on **Choose**, and it will be displayed in the **Package file** field, as shown in the following, rather long, screenshot.

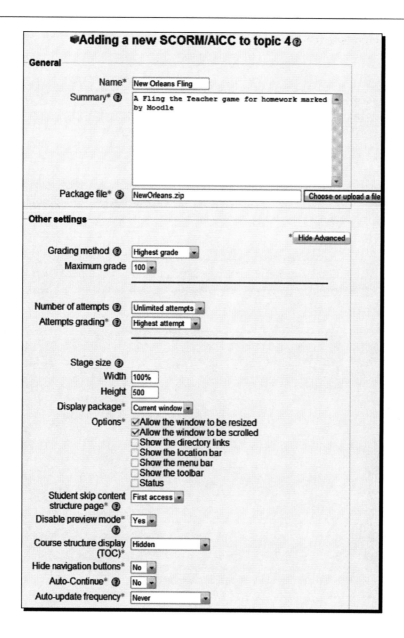

6. Set your options to be the same as the ones shown in the preceding screenshot (if you're missing some options, click on **Advanced** to reveal them).

 SCORM types of activity, like this one, need several files to work, and are quite complex. Fortunately, we don't need to understand any of those files to get them onto our Moodle site. Just ensure that your settings are the same as mine, and your teacher will get flung into your grade book—no problem.

Have a go hero-playing the game

Now that you've completed the complex part, you get to do the fun part—checking if everything works by playing the game! If you go back to the course page, you'll see that our game has its own icon next to it—a bit like a box—which indicates that it is a SCORM activity (for those who really want to know). Click on this icon to play the game. When you get the first question and choices of answer, you'll notice that you also have three lives, unlike the other games we have created.

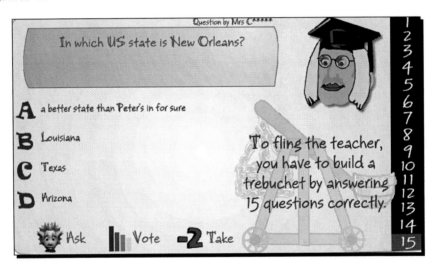

You have to get all fifteen questions correct in order to build the trebuchet and fling the teacher. As soon as you get one answer wrong, the game stops. You'd be amazed (or maybe not!) at how many students will play the game again and again until they get all of the questions correct, in order to do the dirty deed. Eventually, while the students think that they're just playing, we know that by repeatedly checking the answers, they are memorizing the facts!

Once the game is over, you can check the students' scores by clicking on the **Grades** option—which is available on the course admin page. You will see the results displayed as shown in the following screenshot:

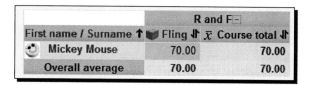

	R and F	
First name / Surname ↑ 📖	Fling ↓↑ $\bar{x}$	Course total ↓↑
🔵 Mickey Mouse	70.00	70.00
Overall average	70.00	70.00

There are more games, like Fling the Teacher, available on the Internet. Fling The Teacher is a free game for all teachers to use. If you like it, you can find similar free games, plus some good value paid-for games, on the web site `http://www.contentgenerator.net/`. You can play soccer, have a swordfight, play Teacher Invaders, and more. Now that you know how to make the games work in Moodle's grade book, you'll have no problem with adding extra activities.

Summary

In this chapter, we've consolidated pupils' knowledge of our rivers and flooding topics by creating five free games for the students to enjoy. We have:

◆ Created two games, entirely online, and linked them into our Moodle course page by using **Add a Resource | Link to a file or website**.

◆ Created two other games that we downloaded and then, by changing a special (.xml) file, we customized it for our purposes. We then uploaded the folder containing this file into Moodle, and linked to the .html file that displays our game.

◆ Generated a fifth game, which we downloaded, added questions to, and then uploaded in a special way that ensures that the results are saved in Moodle.

So far, so good! In this chapter and the previous one, we have used other people's creativity for our own teaching purposes. But what about being creative ourselves? And what about bringing out the creativity of our own students? In the next chapter, we shall do just that, using Moodle as our showcase.

6
Multimedia

This chapter is all about Sound and Vision. A big plus for us, as teachers using Moodle, is that we're not just tied to displaying worksheets that we've had for years. Our classes can watch movies, listen to interviews or stories, and even make their own audio visuals for other students to enjoy. As part of our Rivers and Flooding project, we're going to get our students involved in producing content for Moodle, and we're also going to be creative ourselves.

In this chapter, we shall:

- Make a sound recording of one of our students reading a rivers poem, when they perform an assignment in Moodle
- Make a short film about a field trip our class went on, using students' photos and a narrative read by another member of the class
- Upload the recording and the short film into Moodle to show the students' parents, how talented they are

The term **multimedia** is applied to many ways of communicating. People learn in different ways: some prefer to listen, some prefer to read, and some prefer to watch and learn. We take care in our classroom to cater to different learning styles by adapting our teaching methods to suit both Jane who is a visual learner and Johnny who is a kinesthetic learner. So if we can use different ways to communicate our subjects, then we are more likely to hit the target with our pupils. Within Moodle, we can use multimedia to give variety to the tasks that we set. In this chapter, we're going to use the mediums of sound and video.

Making a sound recording to put into Moodle

Perhaps you have an iPod or an MP3 player. Maybe you download music or talk shows. The files you listen to, or download, are similar to what we are going to create for Moodle. Some people call them podcasts, and although our creations are not podcasts in the strictest terms, we're pretty close!

How do we do it? Well, we need a script to be read out. For that we shall use a poem written by Jamie, a ten year old student in my class. All we need now is the equipment and an instrument to record him with. We need two, or possibly three, items:

1. A computer.

2. A microphone, if your computer doesn't have one built-in.

3. A free program called **Audacity**, which we'll download in a moment.

You don't need an expensive broadcasting-standard furry microphone at all; a basic mike that gets plugged into your computer will do the job for us. You should find a socket with an icon of a mike somewhere at the back or sides of your computer or laptop that you can plug the microphone into.

Time for action-getting Audacity

We need a software program for recording sounds. Let's download a software program Audacity. It is a free open source program for recording and editing sounds.

1. If you already have Audacity installed (some teachers might have it installed on their school computers), then you can skip the first two steps.

2. Go to the web site `http://audacity.sourceforge.net/`.

3. If you are running Windows, click on the **Download Audacity** link. This will have numbers next to it for the latest version; at the time of writing, this was 1.2.6. If you have a Mac, click on **Other downloads**.

4. Follow the instructions on the next screen; the download will start automatically.

5. When the download has finished, go back to the web site, `http://audacity.sourceforge.net/download/windows`.

6. Click on the **Lame MP3 encoder** link, and follow the instructions on the next screen.

What is the Lame MP3 encoder? The best format of the sound file for us to put into Moodle is an MP3 file— the format of songs you might like to listen to and download. In order for **Audacity** to save our recordings in MP3 format, we need to download this oddly-named piece of kit. A nuisance, but we only need to do it once!

The Audacity logo looks as shown in this screenshot. I have mine as a shortcut on my desktop. What we need now, is our microphone (if needed), a quiet place to record (if there is such a place in your school!), and our voice—Jamie—and we are ready to go!

What just happened?

We just downloaded, from the Internet, a free program that allows us to record audio, directly onto our computer. We also downloaded an add-on that will enable us to save our recordings as MP3 files—the most popular format to put on Moodle.

Time for action-setting up to record

We have downloaded the software application named Audacity for the purpose of recording audio. Now, let's set up the Audacity application.

1. Click on the **Audacity** logo. Don't worry about the complex-looking screen; we only need to use a couple of the features.

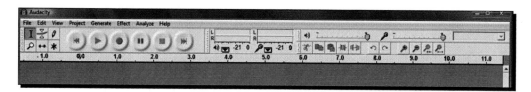

2. Make sure your computer's sound is switched on. Check the loudspeaker icon on the bottom right corner of your screen. If it has a red X, it's off. Click on that icon to turn the loudspeaker on.

3. Click on the red recording circle and speak out loud. If you are able to see sound waves on the screen, as shown in the following screenshot, you have an inbuilt microphone. You can move on to step 8.

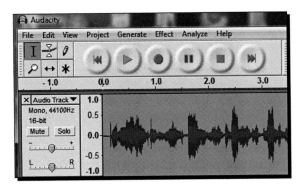

4. If you don't have an inbuilt microphone, you'll need to connect an external microphone. If you have an external microphone, plug it into the computer now, making sure that it's turned on.

5. Go to menu option **Edit | Preferences | Audio I/O**.

6. Now, click on menu option **Recording | Devices | Audio I/O** and select the name of your microphone, and then click on **OK**.

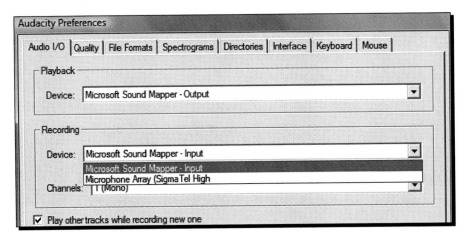

7. Next, click on the red Record button. Speak, and check whether you get the sound waves this time.

8. Look at the size of the sound waves when you pressed the red button to record. They need to be in the range of 0.5 and 0. If the range is anywhere above or below this range, your sound will be too loud or too quiet.

Have a go hero-recording audio

It's over to you now! If you've still got **Audacity**, which we used for our trial run, up on your window click on the **X** button to the left of the **Audio Track**, as shown in the following screenshot. Clicking on the **X** button will clear your screen. Now, be ready to record yourself, or in our case, Jamie!

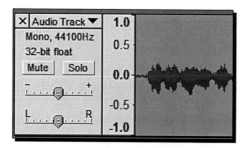

Check that Jamie is neither too near nor too far from the microphone. Click on the red Record button to start recording. Click on the square Stop button to stop. You can pause to gather breath by clicking on the Pause button—available in between the Record and the Stop buttons (the buttons are similar to the buttons on DVD or video players—aren't they?)

Improving the recording and involving our class

If we're happy with the recording, once we've pressed the stop button, we can save it and that's about it. But sometimes, it isn't that simple. Thus, in this section, we'll have a very quick look at how we can improve our sound file. Audacity gives us lots of options for all types of fancy sound effects. We can disguise our voice by speeding up or slowing down the recording. We can also add an echo effect, sound effect, or background music to the recorded voice. The creative possibilities of Audacity would make up a book on their own. Thus, we cannot do them justice in just one part of our chapter. If you ever have time to play with the other controls, do so—the fun results would be worth it! But if you can't set aside the time, why not make Audacity a class project for your students to perform, and upload their productions into the Moodle? We recorded one student, just to become familiar with the program. Why not now pass the buck onto the rest of the class and get them to record their poems themselves? The youngest students I have practiced this method on have been 12 years old. However, I firmly believe that with careful instructions, children younger than this could succeed, too. The main advantage that the students have over us is that they will not be afraid to play with the other controls. Eventually, the students could well produce podcasts of a higher standard than ours, with more imaginative effects.

Time for action-getting rid of the coughs and giggles

Let's just look at a few ways to enhance our effort, and then we'll put the audio recording into Moodle.

1. Play the audio, which you have recorded, by clicking on the green Play button.

2. Find the part of the recording with the cough, giggle, or any other error that you want to cut out from the recording.

3. Use your mouse to select that bit of the file, just as you would highlight a word when typing. In the following screenshot, you'll find that the chosen section is darker:

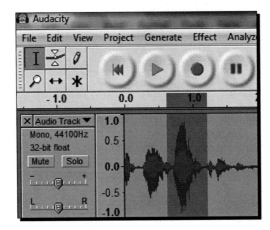

4. Press the *Delete* button on your keyboard, or click on the scissor icon on the Audacity toolbar. Done!

Time for action-adding background music

Now that we have removed all of the imperfections in our recording, let's make it a bit more interesting by adding some background music.

 Although it's tempting to rip our students' chart-topping favorites off a CD and add them to our podcast, copyright rules just don't allow us to do this. We can have up to 30 seconds of professional music, but if our track is long, it's safer (and nicer for our students) to record and use music they've made themselves. Alternatively, we can go to the Creative Commons web site, `http://creativecommons.org`, and search for a suitable music track there.

Let's assume that for Jamie's poem we have a music file already created for us by one of the music classes. It should end in .mp3 or .wav. What next?

1. Select menu option **Project | Import Audio**.

2. Browse for the music file that you want to be played.

3. Select it, and click on **Open**.

4. The file will appear underneath the track that we've just selected. Don't worry if there are two extra tracks.

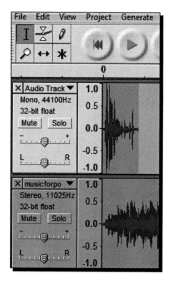

5. Shorten the music file length, if necessary, by using the cough or giggle deletion method.

6. Click on the green Play button and listen to the music along with the voice.

7. To make the background music quieter, go to the music track and move the slider towards the –, and away from the + sign. You can see this in the previous screenshot. To make the music louder, reverse the process. Test it by clicking on the Play button and then re-adjusting the background music level until you are satisfied.

8. Select menu option **File | Save project as**, and give the project a name.

What just happened?

We've just created our first voice recording using Audacity. We got Jamie to record his poem, which we then edited to cut out the bits of the recording that we did not want. And then, to improve the audio recording further, we imported some background music, made it fit the length of the poem, and reduced the volume of the imported music so that it didn't drown out Jamie's voice. We then saved the entire recording as a project file.

This means that, if we want to go back and improve the audio recording another time (change the music and add some effects) we can open the recording up again and edit it. But, if we're going to have a finished podcast ready for Moodle, we should **export** it (the term Audacity uses) as an MP3 file. The first time that we do this we'll get a message asking us to locate the Lame MP3 encoder that we downloaded at the beginning of this chapter. Hopefully, you can remember to where you downloaded the file, and are able to select it. Later on, the procedure will be the same each time that we create our masterpiece.

Time for action-saving our recording

We have created the audio recording with the help of Audacity. Now, we need to upload it into our Moodle course, for which we have to first save it into our computer.

1. Go to **File | Export as MP3**.
2. You'll be directed to your hard disk drive. Find a place to save your file on the hard disk, and give it a name.
3. If you get a message saying that the computer is saving your tracks into one single track, just agree!
4. When the box shown in the following screenshot appears, add the required information about the file, and then click on the **OK** button.

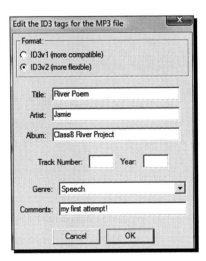

We did it! We have created our sound recording! And more importantly, we now have the skills to show the students how to make their own recording. Why not play the file now and see how it sounds? Then, we'll look at two ways of playing it into Moodle.

Have a go hero-displaying our MP3 file on Moodle

Let's upload the audio recording file, which we have saved on our computer, into our Moodle Course.

- ◆ With editing turned on, select menu option **Add a Resource | Link to a File or Website**
- ◆ **Browse** for, and **Upload** Jamie's recording
- ◆ Choose the poem recorded by Jamie
- ◆ Click on **Save and return to course**

Hopefully, you will have noticed that what seemed like a very tedious affair the first time we uploaded our creation into Moodle has now become much less of an effort, through practice.

If you're satisfied with displaying Jamie's poem in the way you have, stop here and have a coffee. It's fine! If you want to be a bit smarter, read on.

 You can play the MP3 files, and the movies we're about to create, in their own neat little players—like the ones you see on YouTube and other web sites. However, your admin needs to have Moodle set up for this purpose—check with them first. Ask them "whether the multimedia plugin filters are enabled for `.mp3` and `.wmv`". If they say yes, you can do the next bit!

Time for action-adding a link to the audio file

Want your Moodle course to display your audio file as shown in the following screenshot? Follow the instructions under the screenshot! Let's see how to upload Jamie's podcast into the course files of your Moodle course.

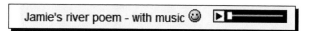

1. Click on the **Turn editing on** button.
2. Under **Add a Resource**, select **Label**.
3. Type in some words to introduce the MP3 file and then press the space bar a few times.

4. Select that empty space, as shown in the following screenshot. Yes, really! Trust me!

5. Click on the **Insert Web Link** icon on the toolbar to create a hyperlink, as shown in the previous screenshot. The white space is highlighted in my screenshot, and I'm about to link it to the podcast.

6. In the dialog box that comes up, navigate to the course file for your audio recording (Jamie's poem, in our case) and select it.

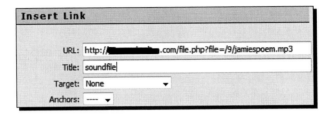

7. Click on **OK**, and then click on **Save and Return to Course**.

8. Hey Presto! One really cool player with hardly any effort at all!

What just happened?

We have recorded our audio file and uploaded it into Moodle. Then, we uploaded Jamie's podcast into the course files of our Moodle course. Finally, we created a hyperlink to the podcast of our recorded audio.

Making a film to put into Moodle

So we can do sound. Now, let's do both sound and vision! If you recall Chapter 3, one of the ways in which we used a database or a glossary was by enabling students to upload resources for others to see and use. If we asked them to upload their favorite photos of our class trip to a river into a Moodle database, we could make use of the pictures in the movie that we're about to create. With our new-found expertise in Audacity, we shall get one of the gang of students to record the narrative, and we shall add that to our movie. Students and parents (who have given permission for their offspring to be featured in the movie) will love to see the action, and it will give the next year's hopefuls an insight into what the trip might entail.

Although we are actually making a movie (in this instance, an animated slideshow) of an event, don't think that's all you could do. With selective usage of images and text, you could create a short film to introduce a new topic. I have seen the **What Happens Next?** movies on Moodle, where the story stops at a crucial point, leaving its climax open to lively discussion. A movie doesn't just have to be something to be watched; it can also be something to be learned from.

And of course, movie-making for Moodle isn't a skill restricted to the teacher! I have often booked two lessons of one hour in a computer room with classes of thirteen-year olds. In the first session, I teach the students the basics of movie-making and in the second hour, I set them an **Upload a single file** assignment, whereby they have to research, produce, and upload a movie on our current topic. We could work and create a movie on the Tsunami of 2004, for example. The students really enjoy it, as it makes a pleasant change from being asked to complete Word-processed tasks or prepare slideshows. Thus, just as with our podcast above, once you've got the hang of film creation, why not pass on this new found knowledge to the students and let them do a better job than you did!

For movie making, we're going to need:

1. A computer with **Windows Movie Maker** installed on it.

2. Some photographs that we have permission to use.

3. A sound to record (in our case, a child recollecting the story of our trip to the river).

It wouldn't be a bad idea to also have a cup of coffee and a cookie with you. Well, these are not essential, but I guarantee that you'll find this a rather relaxing and a creative experience—not like real work at all!

 Windows Movie Maker is a free movie-editing program that comes installed as standard on modern PCs and laptops running Microsoft Windows. The XP and Vista Operating System versions vary slightly, but not by too much. Mac users have their own excellent free program called i-movie, but as most schools tend to use Personal Computers, we shall make our film using Movie Maker.

Time for action-creating our movie

Assuming that we have the **Windows Movie Maker** installed on our computer, let us:

1. Find and open **Windows Movie Maker** on your computer. It is usually located in **All Programs | Accessories | Entertainment | Windows Movie Maker**. However, sometimes, it might simply be located in **All Programs | Windows Movie Maker**.

2. Don't be put off by the complex look of the next screen. Consider it in four parts:

- ❏ On the left, we have a list of tasks.

- ❏ In the middle, we have an image storage area.

- ❏ On the right, we have the preview screen.

- ❏ At the bottom, we have the film strip (timeline or storyboard) to which we'll add our images, subtitles, and commentary.

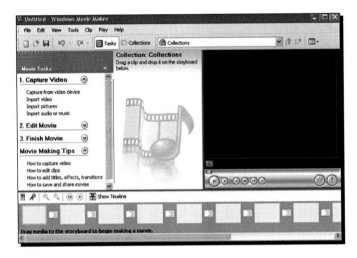

3. Click on the **Import Pictures** link in the list of tasks. You'll be taken to your hard disk drive, from where you can select the photos that you want to add to the movie.

4. If you want to include all of the images from one folder, click on *Ctrl* and *A*.

5. Click on the **Import** button as shown in the following screenshot:

6. The images will now appear in the middle section of the Movie Maker screen, where the images are held.

7. Select one of the images (it doesn't have to be your first photo) with your cursor and drag it onto the first box of the film strip (or the storyboard). It will show on the preview screen on the right.

8. Click the Play button under the preview screen, on the right. Your image will play in a movie for five seconds, and then the screen will go blank. You need more photos!

Have a go hero-adding photos to the movie and testing it out

Over to you now! Select and drag the other photos into the storyboard boxes in the order in which you want them to appear in the movie. If you include the wrong image, press *Delete* on your keyboard. Then select the image that you want to appear first, press Play on the preview screen as before, and watch your movie play!

What just happened?

We used a free program, **Windows Movie Maker**, to make a film of a class trip to a river. We imported some still pictures—that our pupils had taken—into the program, dragged them onto a timeline, and then clicked on the Play button to preview the movie and see how it looks so far.

Improving our movie with effects and sound

Theoretically, we are done now. We can save the movie and upload it into Moodle. How quick and easy is that? But in reality, we would like to add that commentary and make it run a bit more smoothly. As you played your movie through, you probably noticed that it jerked a bit as it went from one photo to another. We can fix that. In fact, we can make the transition—from one picture to another—as simple or as sophisticated as we want. Here's how to do all this.

Time for action-adding special effects to our movie

There are two types of enhancements that we can add: **Transitions**, which make the move from one image to another, and **Effects**, which are fancy features that can be applied to our movie—such as zooming in or out, or making it look like an old, grainy film. Let's add a transition together, and then you can have a go at adding an effect.

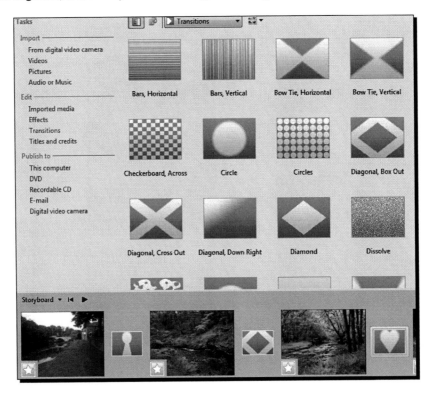

1. From the list on the left, click on **Transitions**.

2. In the middle section of the screen, a wide selection of transitions from which you can choose will be displayed.

3. Select one transition method, with the help your cursor, and drag it into the box between the two images on the storyboard. Three different methods are shown in the previous screenshot.

4. Click the Play button under the preview screen to see how the transition works.

5. Add transitions between each of your images, if you wish. If you have to change your choice, click on the transition and press *Delete* on your keyboard.

You can have lots of fun with transitions, but beware! Too many transitions can spoil a movie rather than enhance it. I tend to use just one throughout, usually the **Fade** effect, which moves smoothly from one image to the next. The same will apply to any effects that you might want to add. Sometimes less is more!

Have a go hero-make your movie zoom in and change color!

You can use just two of the many effects that are available! If you choose effects from the list on the left, you'll get a similar selection in the middle. For a single transition, you click on one transition with your cursor. But this time, you drag it onto the star located at the lower-left of the image that you want it to work on. Try a **Zoom In** and a **Greyscale** and preview them. Fun, isn't it?

Once we're satisfied with our choice of transitions and effects, it's time for us to add the sound. When we do this, we will change the look of the film strip or the storyboard at the bottom. It will become a timeline, but not to worry, that doesn't matter. Remember, for our movie, we are using a pre-recorded (with Audacity) MP3 file of one of our girls poetically describing the trip to the river. The process would be the same if you were using some music file that you had—but keep in mind the points about copyright mentioned earlier in this chapter. **Windows Movie Maker** accepts different types of sound files, but the most common ones you might want to use will have .mp3, .wav, and .wma extensions. Sadly, you can't use your iTunes songs.

Time for action-adding sound to our movie

We have added images and effects to the image transition, but something still seems to be missing. Oh yes! How can a movie be complete without voice? Let's learn how to add sound to our movie.

1. From the list of tasks on the left, choose **Import | Audio or Music**.

2. Select the track you want to add from your computer's hard disk drive.

3. Choose the track, and then click on **Import**, just as you did with the pictures. The imported sound file will appear in the middle section of the **Windows Movie Maker** screen, along with your images.

4. On the lower-left, press the drop-down arrow next to the **Storyboard**, and select **Timeline**.

5. Select the sound clip with your cursor and drag the sound clip to the part of the timeline called **Audio/Music**.

6. You will be able to see the track underneath all of the images.

7. Click the Play button under the preview screen to watch and listen to your movie.

What just happened?

We've added a soundtrack to our movie by finding and **importing** an MP3 file, and then dragging it to the **Audio/Music** section of our movie's timeline. We can move it to the start and end it wherever we want to. However, if the audio clip is too long for our movie, we might have a problem.

Getting the sound to match our images

What if our soundtrack lasts longer than our pictures do? Of course, we can add more pictures, but what if we don't have any more pictures? Well, if it is a music clip, we can:

◆ Either edit it in Audacity to be the correct length and the correct bit of music and then re-import it

◆ Or go to the end of the music clip, click on it, and drag it to the location where the images end, as shown in the following screenshot:

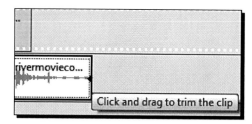

But, as it is our pupil speaking, we don't want to lose any of her lovely narrative. So, we're going to stretch out the pictures instead.

Click on an image—just as you did with the sound file—and drag it out. You'll see the number of seconds it runs for (**Duration**) increase as you drag it. Do this with all of the images until they fit the commentary.

What if our pictures last longer than our soundtrack? We can't stretch out sound as we do with still images. If it's music, we can edit it in Audacity to fit the length of the images by repeating a certain section of the music. Drag the same sound file in again, and set it to play twice (or more times).

Instead, we can click on an image and drag it inwards to make the image play for less time to shorten the audio length. However, the best method is to have just enough images and just the right length of commentary for our movie to look good. That's something that takes practice, trial, and error.

 Did you notice that when you switched from **Storyboard** to **Timeline**, there was an option called **Narrate Timeline**? You can actually record a commentary as the movie is playing if you want—certainly easier for synchronizing the sound and images. We aren't going to do that here, as we've done ours in Audacity, but it's worth giving it a try some other time. Or setting it as a task for the class!

Adding the finishing touches to make our movie ready for Moodle

We are almost there! It would be nice to have opening and closing credits, just like a real movie. Then we need to save it in a way that it will work in Moodle. Let's do that now!

Time for action-adding our opening credits

To make the movie even more interesting, let's add an opening credit and a closing credit.

1. From the list on the left, choose **Titles and credits**.
2. Choose the option **Title at the beginning**, and type in the title of the movie

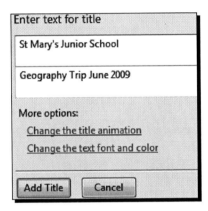

3. Watch it in the preview screen.
4. To change the way it runs, click on the **Change the title animation** link.
5. To change the type, color and size of the text, click on the **Change the text font and color** link.
6. Click on **Add Title**.

 Did you notice that when you first clicked on titles and credits there were four options? Although we are just creating opening and closing credits here, you can also add captions to the actual images, or before each individual image. This is perhaps something for you and your class to experiment with in future movie creation sessions!

And now it is once more over to you.

Have a go hero-adding our closing credits

Adding closing credits works in exactly the same way as adding opening credits. You can follow the same steps as you carried out for the opening credit. However, once you reach step 2, choose **Credits at the end**. You can even have your name rolling up the screen if you wish!

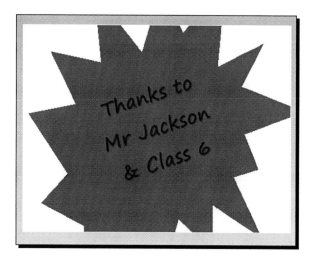

What just happened?

We used **Windows Movie Maker**'s titles and credits feature to add a beginning and an end to our movie. We learned how to type in our own text and then personalize its color, font, size, and the way it runs in the movie.

It's now time to save the movie and upload it into Moodle. The first task can be done by us, together. However, the second can be done by you on your own!

Time for action-saving and uploading the movie into Moodle

We should really save our movie twice: once as a project file in case we want to edit it another time, as we did in Audacity, and again as a proper movie file for Moodle.

1. Go to **File | Save Project As...** and give your movie a name. This will be the project (draft) version, which you can edit again. This should end in .MSWMM and will work only on your own computer.

2. Follow the instructions given in the following table to save the file as a finished movie.

The save process is slightly different according to which version of **Windows Movie Maker** you are using, and the Operating System that you are using—Windows XP or Vista. Either way, your finished file must end in .wmv.

Windows Vista	Windows XP
From the list of tasks on the left, choose **Publish**.	From the list of tasks on the left, choose **Finish Movie	Save to my computer**.
Name it. Browse to where you want to save it, and click on **Next**.	Name it. Browse to where you want to save it, and click on **Next**.
Select **Compress to**.	Click on **Show more choices	Other settings**.
Check whether the **Estimated file space** required is less than your Moodle's maximum upload limit. If not, move the compress number down.	Choose the option **Video for broadband 512 kbps**.
Click on **Publish**.	Click on **Next** to save your movie.

Have a go hero-displaying our movie in Moodle

No need for any more step-by-step instructions because if you can upload the MP3 file we made with Audacity, you can upload a movie too. It's done in exactly the same way. Do you remember that there were two ways to do it?

1. The first method was to go to **Add a resource | Link to a File or Web site | Link to the Movie**.

2. The second method was (if your Moodle is set up for this) to go, **Add a resource | insert a label**, and then selecting some blank spaces and linking it to your movie with the help of the **Inset Web link** option. If you choose this option, it will display in a player—for example, video sharing web sites such as Youtube.

Summary

In this chapter, we've have taken a look at how to use multimedia to showcase our students' work. We've learned how to:

♦ Create, edit, and upload a sound file of a student reading a poem into Moodle

♦ Create, edit, and upload a film of a school trip into Moodle

♦ Play our sound recording or movie in two different ways, bearing in mind their appearance

Additionally, and very importantly, we've also learned the basics of two programs, **Audacity** and **Windows Movie Maker**, which we can now share with our class students to inspire them to be creative. Remember the old Native American proverb:

"Tell me and I'll forget. Show me and I might not understand. Involve me and I'll remember".

In the next chapter, we shall consider more ways of using Moodle to involve our students' with a rich choice of options from the world of Web 2.0.

7
Wonderful Web 2.0

In the olden days (known as Web 1.0), the Internet was all about emails and web sites, developed by professionals, with pages of text that you scrolled down to read. Nowadays, the Internet is for anybody and everybody who can get in on the act. Have you ever watched videos on YouTube? Seen photos on Flickr? Maybe even uploaded some yourself? Are you on Facebook or Myspace? Then you're already in the Web 2.0 world; joining in is what it's all about! In this chapter, we shall look at some Web 2.0 applications that can be used in Moodle—both by us, the teachers, and by our students. Remember—they were born into this world, so let's harness what they're used to!

In this chapter, we're going to link geography with literacy and set our students a project imagining how they'd react if their home town were flooded. We shall:

- Get the students to keep a blog of their experience as they work through the project
- Set up a Google Map of the riverside area that we're focusing on
- Enjoy converting ourselves into a talking animated character to introduce the project
- Let the students make an animation cartoon of their experience
- Give the students a chance to summarize their project with a word cloud

All of the above activities are examples of Web 2.0 applications. They are free to use, and also easily to fit into Moodle. What's more, they are a lot of fun! We'll make a start imminently, but let's first understand a few basic concepts.

Web 2.0 words of warning

Apart from the Moodle blog, the rest of this chapter is about bringing the **World Wide Web (www)** inside our protected walled garden, that is, Moodle. Along with the immense potential that Web 2.0 brings to us come possible dangers, especially for our younger students. Thus, each of my suggestions will come with a few **words of warning**. This is not to put you off in anyway, but just to help you make informed decisions about whether to use these tools.

Getting the pupils to Blog!

The word **blog**, apparently, comes from Web + log, and a blog is just an online diary or journal. Blogs are a very commonly used Web 2.0 application, and there are many blogs around. But we don't need to go outside of Moodle, as every user has his or her own space to blog, as part of their user profile. If you log into Moodle and then click on your name, you'll see what I mean:

Students have these tabs too, and they operate in just the same way as ours. So let's set the ball rolling by creating the first **Blog** entry (which our students will see), and get them blogging in return:

Time for action-introducing our project with a blog entry

Let's create an introduction to our project, with the help of a blog entry:

1. Click on your profile, as above, and then click on the **Blog** tab, as shown in the preceding screenshot.

2. Click on **Add a new entry**.

3. Type a title in the **Entry title** box, and your blog entry in the **Blog entry body**, as shown in the following screenshot:

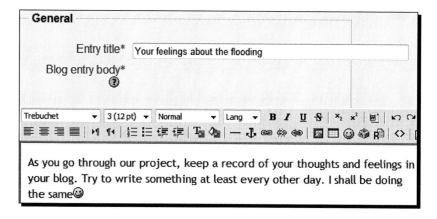

4. Scroll down, and in the option **Publish To**, choose **anyone on this site**.

5. Click on **Save changes**.

What just happened?

We used the blogging facility in our profile on Moodle to make a blog entry to introduce the new project to our pupils. We can add to it as we go along, specifying exactly what we'd like the students to do.

Words of warning

These are really warnings, just a couple of issues that you need to be aware of.

- In Moodle, blogs are attached to people, not courses. Thus, if you click on somebody's username in Moodle, you will usually see their blog. Be aware, then, that the blogs in your students' profiles (and your own) aren't private within your Moodle.

- You might be wondering about **Tags**, as you scroll down to save your blog entry. Basically, a tag is a word connected to your interests (for us, it might be flooding) and it will link to other people on Moodle with that same tag or interest. Moodle also lets you add a tag for one of your interests and then link this to a selection of related YouTube videos or Flickr photos. However, some schools have Youtube and Flickr banned because of the possibly unsuitable content. Other schools switch off 'tags' in case students decide to use inappropriate words. On the plus side, however, your Moodle admin can add a block showing tags, if you wish, and these tags or 'keywords' can provide a quick and easily updatable reference list of what's currently popular.

Putting a map onto Moodle

Now, our blog is up and running. What we need to do now is set the scene of the project by studying a map of the area concerned. We're going to avoid paper maps. I can never fold them back properly and my pupils are even worse! Instead, we'll use a Google Map and embed it (paste it) into Moodle. Even better, if you don't live too far from a river, you can use your own home town—they'll identify with it much better. So here goes:

Time for action-how to display a Google Map on our course page

Let's learn how to grab and display a Google Map on our Moodle course page:

1. Go to the Google Maps web site, `http://maps.google.com`, and in the **Search Maps** option, type either your chosen location or a zip or postal code.

2. Once you are happy with your choice, click on the **Link** button, which is present at the top right of your Google Map screen, as shown in the following screenshot.

3. Click inside the option **Paste HTML to embed in website** (and don't worry about all the strange wording coming up!), and copy the text in it.

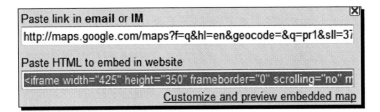

 Remember, you can select the entire text by pressing *Ctrl+A*. You can copy by pressing *Ctrl+C*. You can paste by pressing *Ctrl+V*.

4. Go to your course page on Moodle, and click on **Turn editing on**.

5. Click on the **Add a resource...** menu and choose the **Compose a text page** option.

6. In the **Name** field, type the name of the map that your students need.

7. In the **Compose a text page** box, paste (*Ctrl + V*) the text that you copied from Google Maps.

8. In the **Format** box, choose **HTML format**.

9. Click on **Save and return to course**. Done!

If we now click on the name that we have given to the map—in this instance, **flooding area**—it opens up a new page with our map pasted (embedded) straight from Google.

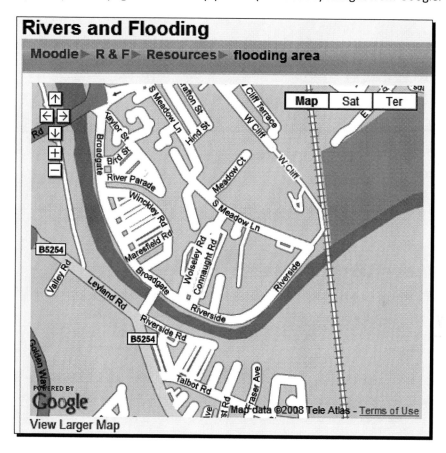

But this is not just a static map! Your students can move the map around and zoom in, just as they would if they were using Google maps directly from the Internet. They can look at the satellite image instead of the conventional map. And in fact, if you make yourself a Google account you can add place marks, images, and even videos to the bit of the map that you are showing. However, that's not for this book to explain, but it's something to look at once you've mastered Moodle.

What just happened?

We located a map on Google of the area we're studying. We got its web site link and pasted it into a text page on Moodle. As a result, the map is displayed, along with all of its features, for our students to examine.

 Embedding code from web sites is not that hard, and you'll find that many so-called Web 2.0 applications work in a similar way. You merely copy and paste the code that they offer into your Moodle page to get them to show up. We're talking transferable skills!

Words of warning

This, again, is not really a warning, just something to be aware of when you embed maps.

Your class will love having Google maps in Moodle. Unfortunately, once they discover all of the possibilities, you might well find them distracted from the task that you set. I once embedded a map of our school, and found that within a few minutes, the students had moved the map from our school to their own streets and were zooming in on the satellite view of their homes. So rather than reprimand them, I used their inclined interest as the starting point for a lesson on navigating with Google maps. But you do need to be vigilant!

Introducing the project with a cartoon character

It's much more fun to set out a task with a moving and talking character than to give instructions in a wordprocessed document, or even by a Moodle assignment that I was encouraging you to do in Chapter 2. We're going to make a character (or Avatar) online and, using the same principle as with the Google Map above, we are going to paste or embed it into a Moodle page. We are going to use a free site where we shall make a Voki:

Time for action-creating a moving and a talking teacher

Let's create an animated, moving, and talking, teacher and make our Moodle course learning even more enjoyable to the students.

1. Go to the web site `http://www.voki.com/` and create yourself a free account.

2. Click on **Create A New Voki**, as shown in the following screenshot:

3. You will see an image and several boxes with options for editing your character.

4. In the **Customize Your Character** option, click on the **HEAD** tab. Click on the right and left arrows to choose the type of character that you want to start with (**CLASSIC** are the most 'conventional' types). Select the gender of the character, **MALE** or **FEMALE**.

5. Scroll down to see the choices available; click on the one that you want.

6. Your chosen character will appear in the large screen to the left. Alter its features by using the **Color/Tweak** box shown below.

7. In the **Customize your Character** option, click on the **CLOTHING** tab. As with the **HEAD** tab, click on the right and left arrows to choose the type of clothing you want for the character and then click on the item to finalize it.

8. Do the same for the **BLING** (which includes spectacles) tab.

9. Click on **DONE**, as shown in the preceding screenshot.

10. Next, click on the **Backgrounds** option. Use the arrows of the keyboard, as before, to choose a background, or click on the folder (as shown in the following screenshot) to browse and upload your own image. Click on **DONE**.

11. Now look at the **Give It A Voice** option. We're going to enter the message that is to be spoken by the computer. You can record your message on the phone, on the mike, or make one with Audacity, as we did in Chapter 6.

12. Click on the button with the image of a keyboard button named **T**. Type in your text, as shown in the following screenshot:

13. Select your choice in the options **Accent/Language** and **Voice**, from the menus under the text.

14. Click on the Play arrow available under the text box to test the playback of the written text.

15. Click on **DONE**.

16. In the large screen on the left, click the Play button to preview your character.

17. When you're satisfied with it, click on **PUBLISH**.

18. Give your creation a name by entering this name in the **Name Your Scene** box.

19. Click your cursor inside the box saying **For Most Sites Use This Code:** and copy the words within it (like Google Maps, remember?).

What just happened?

We created an account on a free site called Voki in order to generate a moving and talking character who will explain our project to the students. We chose the character's appearance, and entered the words that we want the character to speak.

Have a go hero-put your Voki onto Moodle!

We've created our moving and talking teacher. Now it is time to put them on our course! If you managed to embed a Google Map into your Moodle course, then you will be able to embed a Voki as well. The process is exactly the same. Click on **Compose a text page**, then paste the code, and select the **HTML format** in the **Format** option. Have a go and do it now! Did you get something similar to the following screenshot?

If you want the Voki to appear immediately as the children access the course (as a welcome message), you can put the code into a label or in topic 0 instead of a text page. Before you paste the code, click on the < > symbol, as shown in the following screenshot.

Words of warning

I have two important warnings for you, this time:

1. When we use web sites that are not connected to Moodle, there is always a possibility that they might not always be available for your course. The web site owner might change the terms and conditions of the site's use, or shut down the site altogether. Web 2.0 moves at a very fast speed. Indeed, some people are even saying that the very term Web 2.0 is old fashioned these days. At the time of writing this book, the web sites that we are using in this chapter are very useful and stable. However, by the time you read this book, there might be other, better ones.

2. Do you see the advertisement underneath my Voki character (which is me, by the way!)? Because we are using a free site, it's going to have advertisements displayed, and you might worry that some are not suitable for younger children's eyes. I have been using Vokis in Moodle ever since they began, and haven't had any problems. My students are used to advertisements all over the Internet, and tend to ignore them and focus on the Voki. The Voki site states that it should not be used by children under the age of 13 so sadly some of your students won't be able to make their own avatars as you have. However, once again, you do need to be aware of the fact that once you are outside the safety of Moodle, there could be inappropriate contents. Our next trip will take us to a web site that is very popular with teachers and students, but where, again, the content could be an issue.

Telling our story through a cartoon animation

We're going to get our class to use an online animation maker to relate their flooding tale. There are several free online cartoon maker web sites. However, the one that we shall use is intuitive to beginners (especially if you are familiar with Windows Movie Maker) and offers a number of templates and soundtracks. Although there is no age limit for the web site, I wouldn't recommend it for pupils under the age of 13 because of the unsuitability of some of the characters. I have had 13 year old students who have made fantastic animations on this site and send me the links in Moodle (as we shall do shortly) with no problems, whatsoever. However, as I mentioned in the previous words of warning, the age limit restriction is a consideration personal to you and your school. I cannot make that decision for you. Look at it yourself and see what you think. While I am working on this book, the site's owners are working on an educational version specifically for school students.

If we're going to set story-telling using cartoon animation as a task for our students, perhaps we should learn how to use it ourselves first! Although, I confess, I only looked at its features very briefly myself before sending my class off on a journey of discovery—instructing them to **play with it** and teach themselves and each other how to animate. So let's take a whistle-stop tour so that we don't look too incompetent in front of our young, soon-to-be-expert animators!

Time for action-creating our animation

We need and create and animate cartoon characters for the purpose of story telling. Let's learn how to animate:

1. Go to the web site `http://www.goanimate.com`.
2. Click on **Sign Up** and make yourself a free account.

 You might want to make yourself an account and let all your students use that. Otherwise, if your students have school email IDs, ensure that they use those. If not, you will need parental permission for the children to use their own personal emails.

3. Click on **Create**.

4. Choose **Blank Slate** (create from scratch), and then click on **Create Now**.

5. From the **Theme** option, choose the type of characters that you'd like to use.

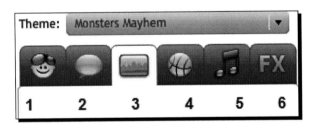

6. Click on the icons shown in the screenshot above, to access the features that I've outlined in the following table:

Icon	What it does
1	You choose your character(s) here, by clicking on the ones that you want, and they'll appear on the screen.
2	Select a speech bubble by clicking on it. When it appears on the screen, click on it to move it around, and then type your text into it.
3	Select a background by clicking here.
4	Click here to get props for your characters. Once clicked, they appear on the screen.
5	There are some soundtracks here. Click on one to add it, and click on it again to alter its length and volume.
6	Click on a special effect to apply it to your scene.

7. Import your own background images and sounds if you wish, by clicking on **My Stuff** and then clicking on **Import**. The screen shown in the screenshot below is displayed.

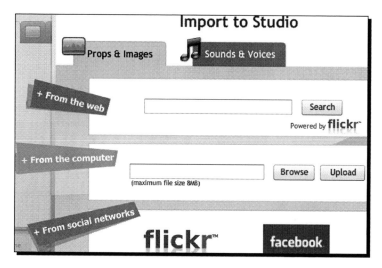

8. Choose the option **From the computer** and, just as with Moodle, browse for your photo or sound file and then click on **Upload**. The uploaded file will then be available for you to select as a background.

We're doing a flooding story. Thus, I decided to use one of our field trip photographs that a student uploaded to a database, which we set up for our movie in Chapter 6. After that, I've added cartoons of a couple of children and speech bubbles. Enough for one scene, I think!

What just happened?

We created an account on a site called **Go! Animate** and made a scene using one of our own photos as a background. We added characters and speech bubbles to begin a flooding story.

Have a go hero-add several scenes to an animation

Give it a try. It's a lot of fun! To add another scene, simply click on the **+** button on the lower-left of the screen. To delete a scene, click on the **−** button.

The **Preview** button above our animation window will enable us to see how the animation plays. If we're satisfied with the outcome, then it's time to upload it into Moodle!

Time for action-saving our animation which is ready for Moodle

Now that we have created the animation, it's time to save it. We can later upload the saved animated file into Moodle.

1. Click on **Save** (next to the preview arrow in the screenshot above).
2. Enter the details of your animation and make sure that you select **Public**.
3. Click on **Save**, and then on **Share**.
4. From the screen that is displayed next, click on the envelope, as shown in the following screenshot.

5. Then, click on **Copy** to copy that code to your clipboard ready for Moodle.

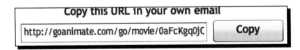

If you want to be really clever in Moodle, you could click on the < > button, and it would give you some web code, similar to what we got for our Google Map and Voki. You could paste this web code into a Moodle text page in exactly the same way. However, our students won't be able to do that easily. Thus, we're going to do it their way, in order to show them how.

Have a go hero-setting up our Moodle animation activity

Yes—your turn! After the students' efforts in making the animation, we need our class to have a simple way of sharing their creation with everyone else. So we're going to set up a forum, of the **single simple discussion** type, and as a first post, we shall include our own animation by simply pasting the link that we just copied. When a student clicks on the link, they get taken to our cartoon on the web site and immediately believe that they can do better.

Therefore, remember how we did this in Chapter 3. With editing turned on, go to **Add an activity...** and then select the option, **A single simple discussion**. Include your instructions and the link to the example animation. Does it look something like the following screenshot?

If it does, well done, and good luck with the animations!

Words of warning

In order to be able to share our animations, we and the children have to make the upload **Public**—that is, we have to allow everyone to view them on the Web. This means that you need to ensure that the students are not including their own photographs or their real names. This could lead to identification of the individual by anyone on the Internet. We can use a landscape image as our background; that still leaves a lot of possibilities open for making the most out of the photographs that the students have clicked.

Summarizing our project in a word cloud

I had said at the start of this chapter, that we'd be combining geography with literacy. With our final Web 2.0 application, our students will not only be doing that but also arguably creating a piece of artwork. We shall be using a tool called **Wordle,** which is a graphic representation of the most frequently used words in a blog, free write, or speech. In simple terms, it is a customizable word picture where the words used most often are the largest. It's become very popular with political analysts who use it to discover the most frequently-used words of election candidates. I have also seen it being used by teachers wishing to review the syllabus of exam boards. They enter the syllabus into Wordle to find out which topics are given more emphasis. However, we're going to use it as a medium of reflection—and also to have fun! As with our previous application, let's first create a sample exercise ourselves, so that we can speak with authority when we set our class off on the task. Do you want to see what I mean? The following screenshot shows my work in Wordle, that I created earlier:

It needs more words really, but I left it simple to encourage my class to do better! So how do we make one?

Time for action-making a Wordle word cloud

Let's learn how to create a Wordle word cloud.

1. Go to the web site `http://www.wordle.net`.
2. Click on the **Create** tab.
3. Type (or paste) your words. The more often you enter a word, the bigger the word cloud will be. Click on the **Go** button.

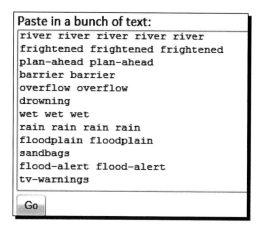

4. Change the font, color, and the layout of your created Wordle by clicking the tabs available above the word cloud, as shown in the following screenshot:

5. When you're satisfied with the word cloud, click on **Save to Gallery**.

6. Copy the link that you get for your Wordle (press *Ctrl+C* on your keyboard).

What just happened?

We used a web site called **Wordle** to make a word cloud of the terms on our topic of flooding. The more often we typed the words, the larger they appeared in the word cloud. We chose a font and color, decided how we wanted our cloud to appear, and then saved it as a link. We will give that to our students.

Have a go hero-getting our students to send us their Wordle word clouds

I guaranteed that your students will get the idea instantly and will be very creative with its appearance. However, we want the students to benefit from this and not just play with it. Thus, we need to make our instructions in Moodle clear to the students. Let's use a forum again, of the single simple discussion type, and let's have the students send us the link to their Wordle, as they had done with their animation. Here's a screenshot that shows the forum for our flooding Wordle:

You're going to use Wordle to make a summary of your thoughts about this project.

- Make a list of TEN words that came to your mind in doing this project
- Now put them in order of importance to you
- When you make your Wordle, write the most important one TEN times
- Write the least important one ONCE
- and the others in between ☺

Paste your link in a forum post. Here's mine but it's not very good ☺
http://www.wordle.net/gallery/wrdl/299477/ourfloodingproject

The students could save the Wordle as an image instead and upload it as an attachment to their forum post. To save the Wordle word cloud as an image, we need to follow a few additional steps:

- Press the *Prt Scr* button on your computer (Windows) when your Wordle is finished
- Go to **All Programs | Accessories | Paint** and press *Ctrl* and *V* on your keyboard to paste your Wordle image
- Go to **File | Save as** and choose `.jpg`
- On a Mac computer, press *Command-Shift-3* to save your image as a `.png` file onto your desktop

Words of warning

Nothing new this time—just a reminder.

When we and our students save the Wordle to the gallery, it becomes visible to the world at large. So names with address or anything incriminating should not be entered. Equally, there will be Wordle images on the site with **inappropriate content** if your students look hard enough. However, many teachers across the globe use Wordle successfully, and I am yet to hear of a student being traumatized by it. But it's your call.

Summary

In this chapter, we mainly ventured outside of the Walled Garden, that is Moodle, and entered the wonderful world of Web 2.0. This has enabled us to add creativity and more interactivity to our Moodle course by:

+ Getting our students to blog from their profile page

+ Embedding a Google Map into our course

+ Creating a moving and a talking teacher with Voki (for a refreshing change from ourselves!)

+ Getting our class to tell a story online, with Go Animate

+ Channeling their literary (and artistic) creativity with Wordle

We've had a lot of fun in the last three chapters. However, if we want to make our Moodle course successful and long-lasting, we need to ensure that everything we put on it actually works for us and our students. Not as obvious as you might assume, but of vital importance. Now that we have got plenty of skills under our belt, in the next chapter, we shall have a look at the practicalities and the nitty-gritty of Moodle!

8
Practicalities

This chapter is about the 'nitty-gritty' of uploading and displaying our stuff in Moodle. We need to ensure that everything works for our pupils and teaching colleagues. I don't mean this in a technical sense with respect to the Internet connection—that's our Admin's job. However, we have to be certain about our worksheets, slideshows, photos, and other resources—all of which should be able to be easily be accessed, regardless of the type of computer that the people use.

In this chapter, we're going to help a student, Joe, who can't view our worksheets and PowerPoint presentations at home. We're also going to advise a colleague, Liz, who is new to Moodle and wants help displaying her teaching materials. We shall:

◆ Provide our students with an alternative way of viewing worksheets and slideshows if they don't have Microsoft Word or PowerPoint

◆ Learn how to display word-processed files in a way everyone can see them

◆ Make it easier for our classes to watch our slideshow presentations

◆ Investigate how best to upload and display photos on Moodle

◆ Find out how to show YouTube videos on our course even though YouTube is banned in school

Miss, I can't do the homework coz I haven't got Word at home!

Many of us, even without thinking about it, create worksheets in Microsoft Office Word and presentations in Microsoft Office PowerPoint. This might be because our school has a license for them and they are installed on our computers. However, they don't always come for free when you purchase a desktop computer or a laptop. Sometimes, you may have to buy them separately. I know several of my students who don't have these programs at home. But I refuse to accept the excuse from our pupil Joe for not having completed his homework, as there is a free alternative! **OpenOffice** is a suite of applications for word processing, spreadsheets, presentations, and so on that anyone can download and use. It is also suitable if you have a Mac instead of a Windows-based computer. If you have OpenOffice, you can view files created in MS Office even though you don't have MS Office. Students can upload their work using OpenOffice's equivalent of Word, and Moodle will be happy to accept them. We're going to download it for use and then put a link to the site on our course page so that the students can download it at home.

 Like Moodle, OpenOffice is also open source. This means that anyone is welcome to help in improving both Moodle and OpenOffice, as the code that makes them work is available for people to adapt and offer to the rest of the world for free. True global collaboration!

Time for action-getting a free alternative to Microsoft Office

Students who don't have MS Office installed in their computer can search the Internet for some software application that supports MS Office created files. One such application is the OpenOffice. Let's learn how to download it.

1. Go to the website `http://www.openoffice.org/`.
2. Click on **I want to download OpenOffice.org**.

 I want to download OpenOffice.org
Download OpenOffice.org for free, or find out about other ways of getting it

3. If you have a Windows PC, click on **Download now!** If you have a Mac computer, click on **Get more platforms and languages** and select your download file from there.

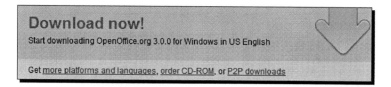

4. If you are using Internet Explorer and you get a message saying that the download is blocked for security reasons, click on the message, and then click on the **download this file**.

5. When the next screenshot comes up, click on **Run** (if you have only the **save file** link, that's ok instead).

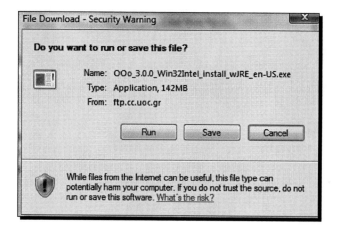

6. If you are prompted to agree to the installation, go ahead and agree.

7. Click on **Next** to install OpenOffice.

8. Click on **Unpack**, then click on **Next** until you get to the following screenshot, and then click **Finish.**

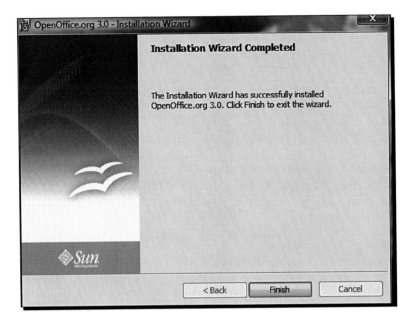

What just happened?

We visited the OpenOffice web site and downloaded a free program that will enable us to word-process documents, make slideshow presentations, and create spreadsheets. The program will let us and our students open the folder and edit the Microsoft files without having Microsoft Office on our computer. For our pupil Joe, and others like him, this can be really handy. His parents don't need to fork out money for him to be able to do his homework on Moodle. His parents just need to let him download the OpenOffice suite! This is where you come in.

Have a go hero-giving our students an alternative to Microsoft Office

Our first step in downloading of OpenOffice was to go to http://www.openoffice.org/. Why not provide a link at the top of our Moodle course? If we do this, the pupils can download the software directly from our Moodle site. You could:

♦ Either edit **Topic 0** and add the link to OpenOffice as a hyperlink

♦ Click on **Add a Resource | Insert a label** and then **Add a resource | link to a file or website** to provide a short description with a link to OpenOffice, as shown in the following screenshot:

> **Rivers and Flooding: What's it all about?**
>
> Click here to go to the National Geographic Kids' Site
>
> *Don't have Word? Don't have Powerpoint? Click the link below!* ☺
> OpenOffice - a free program

OpenOffice works in a very similar way to Microsoft Word, and you and your students will soon get the hang of it. You might notice, however, that when the students send their work to you in a Moodle assignment, the last few letters of the filename (the **file extension**) are different from what we might expect. Let's take a step back for a moment and look at some of the file extensions that our worksheets might have:

File extension	What it is
.doc	A Microsoft Word (such as Word 97 or Word 2003) document.
.docX	A Microsoft Word 2007 document. If you don't have MS Office 2007, you can open it in OpenOffice (if you don't have the 2007 version you can ask the student to save as a 97-2003 file).
.wps	Microsoft Works document. Sometimes, instead of Microsoft Word, this program comes free with new PCs . If you choose **File | Save as** you can save the file as a Word document (you can also download Word Viewer).
.odt	An OpenOffice word-processed document.
.pdf	The sort of file that you have to open with Adobe Acrobat Reader. You can't easily edit it, but it can at least be opened on all computers. (See the following topic for more information.)

Choosing the best file type for Moodle

As I said earlier, uploading our worksheets into Moodle is as simple as we first thought. The situation could be such that we've got Word 2007, but our students only have Word 2003. It could also be that we've got Word 2003, and the students don't have any version of Microsoft Office at all. Or they only have Microsoft Office created documents on their computer, but do not have Microsoft Office installed. Using OpenOffice can be very helpful to you in such cases. However, for us—as teachers—there is another possibility.

Our colleague Liz wants to know the best way to display her worksheets in Moodle, without much effort. Her worksheets are a mixture of .doc, .odt, and .docx depending on the computer she works on. As she wants the students to only view her materials and not download or edit them, what I'd suggest to her is that she save her material as .pdf files.

PDF stands for Portable Document Format, and is a type of file that works on different computers and with different operating systems. Use it if you merely need your students to read a resource and not alter it.

Almost everyone has a program called **Adobe Reader**, which opens these .pdf files. Thus, people will be able to view Liz's materials with no difficulty. Let's look at how Liz (and we) can do this, using a homework resource on the Mississippi, which she has stored as a .docx file.

 Adobe Reader is a software that is usually present on people's computers. Why not provide a link to download it on your course page just like the one that we created for OpenOffice? You should link to http://www.adobe.com/products/reader/.

Time for action-saving a Rivers homework as a pdf file for ease of access on Moodle

As we know, not everybody will have the MS Office software installed on their computer. Thus, for the files that we want the users to only read and not edit, we can save the file as a PDF file. Let's learn how to do this.

1. Open **OpenOffice** on your computer (you might have an icon on the desktop).

2. Click on **Open a document...** and browse and select the file that you want to open using the OpenOffice software just as you would for Moodle.

3. The file will open up in OpenOffice.

4. Click on **File** and then click on **Export as PDF**, as shown in the following screenshot:

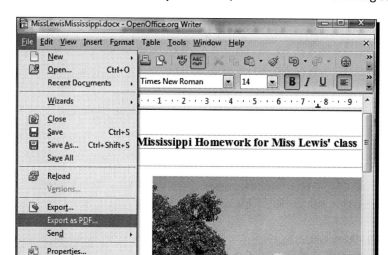

5. On the next screen, click on **Export**.

6. Select where you want the file saved to, and then click on **Save**.

What just happened?

We used a built-in feature of OpenOffice to create a different version of Liz's homework sheet, which can be read on many different types of computer. We opened up the document (that had been created in Microsoft Word 2007) and exported it as a `.pdf` file. You can see the result it in following screenshot:

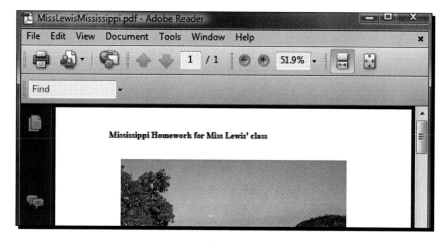

If you don't want to use OpenOffice to create a PDF, you can download a free (Open Source) program called PDFCreator from the web site `http://sourceforge.net/projects/pdfcreator/`. This program acts like a printer. You create your worksheet in a Word document, then instead of choosing your usual (real-life) printer you choose PDFCreator, and it will generate a PDF version of the file for you. Sometimes, when converting documents into PDF, the layout (formatting) changes, so you check this before uploading your file to Moodle. However, I've found that PDFCreator is very good at maintaining the formatting.)

Have a go hero-convert a PowerPoint to a PDF and upload it to Moodle

The same problem that our pupil Joe could have with Word documents could also occur with Microsoft PowerPoint. If he doesn't have PowerPoint on his home computer, and if he hasn't downloaded OpenOffice, he won't be able to see the slideshow presentations. However, OpenOffice will convert these slideshows into .pdf just as quickly. Try it, and then use **Add a resource | Link to a file or website** to upload the PDF file into Moodle!

Making it easier for our students to view our slideshows

Didn't you just do that? Well, yes. One way to ensure that our wonderful presentations are accessible to all our students, irrespective of their home set up, is to convert the presentation into .pdf files. However, a .pdf file is pretty static. It won't include any animations, sound, or video. It basically takes an interactive slideshow and converts it into an online paper version. Not good enough. Our colleague Liz has spent a long time on her PowerPoint presentations, and she is not keen on losing their effects. We're going to work with her on a slideshow that she created on the New Orleans floods, and ensure that it stays as jazzy on Moodle as it is offline! To do this, we shall download yet another free application—which converts PowerPoint slideshows into interactive Macromedia Flash files. You don't need to know anything about Flash to be able to do this. However, it's worth noting that you and your students need to have a recent version of the Flash player installed on your computer in order for the application to work (just as you need Adobe Reader to view PDF files). Let's take it one step at a time.

Time for action-getting a program that displays our interactive presentations

Let's download a program that will convert our PowerPoint slideshows into interactive Flash files.

1. Go to the website `http://www.ispringsolutions.com`.

2. Click on the **Download** button.

3. If you are using Internet Explorer and are prompted to **Run** or **Save**, click on **Run**. If you are using Firefox you will only get the **Save File** option. Click on it, save the file, and then open it.

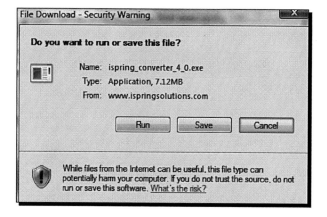

4. If asked whether you want to run the software, agree and **Run**!

5. In the set up wizard, click on **Next**.

6. Agree to the terms and conditions, and then click on **Next** until the software is installed.

7. Click on **Finish**. The application will open up and prompt you to **Launch PowerPoint**.

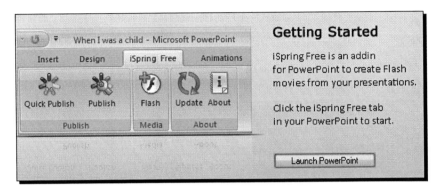

What just happened?

We went to the **iSpring Solutions** web site and downloaded a free program that will convert our PowerPoint presentations to a little Flash movie that will play nicely in Moodle, with all of our animations included. The free program is named **iSpring Free**. In the future, we just need to go to PowerPoint and there will be a toolbar present for us to save our presentation using iSpring.

Time for action-saving our slideshow so that everyone can see it

By everyone I mean all pupils and teachers—whether or not they have MS Office or OpenOffice! We're going to open up Liz's New Orleans PowerPoint slideshow, save it in Flash format, and then upload it into Moodle. Let's learn how it is done.

1. Open up PowerPoint and open the presentation that you want to convert.

2. In the toolbar at the top, click on **Publish**.

3. On the next screen, select or deselect the **Start presentation automatically** option according to your wish.

4. Click on the **Publish** button again.

What just happened?

We've just converted a regular PowerPoint to a fancy Flash movie that will work on all of our pupils' computers! Having downloaded and installed the iSpring program, we simply needed to open up our presentation and publish it into Flash format. You'll find that no matter which format your new file is initially saved in, it will end up in the .swf format. That's yet another file extension, and it tells us that the file it is a Flash file. This is the one to go on our course page.

Have a go hero-uploading and displaying our new slideshow in Moodle

There's nothing magical about this next step. Instead of uploading Liz's PowerPoint slideshow on the New Orleans floods, we're going to upload the .swf file made for us by iSpring. You can try saving a PowerPoint slideshow that you've created (preferably with some animations so that you can see them work). If you use the same file that you earlier converted to .pdf, you'll be able to compare and contrast the two versions. Then go to your Moodle course and click on **Turn editing on**. Then go to menu option **Add a resource | Link to a file or website**, upload the file, and display it. Our New Orleans one looks like this:

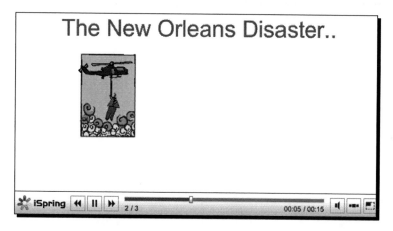

Can you see that the slideshow comes with its own little player? This is neat! Another improvement over displaying it as a regular slideshow is the fact that it opens up with one click and doesn't eat up a lot of the students' time. Using a regular slideshow students might face problems, such as first seeing a message asking **Do you want to open or save this file?**, then having to decide on **Yes** or **No**, then opening the file, and finally discovering that they can't view it because they don't have the correct version of Microsoft PowerPoint.

Making sure that all of our images look correct on Moodle

Haven't we already done this in Chapter 1? Uploaded photos? Yes, but we're just going to do some **tweaking** now—especially, as Liz has some images that she'd like to display. She has a folder of photos from her cousin who was actually involved in this traumatic disaster in 2004. Liz wants to display the folder of photos and wants to use one of them, smaller in size, in the label to introduce her materials. So we need to look at how to resize photos.

It is better to resize your photos before you upload them into Moodle. If you use the **handle** in the HTML editor to resize a photo, the image could appear distorted. If you change its dimensions online, the image might look smaller even though the file size is still as large. Think of it as a song. Both the lyrics as well as the music last only for three minutes. However, if you're told you can have only one minute of music, but you still have to fit in the three minutes of lyrics, it just wouldn't be right, would it? Similarly, if you try to resize your photo once it's uploaded, it would not be right! So we'll do it the proper way.

But first, let's take a quick look at what we actually mean when we say **image**. As with word-processed documents, images can come in different types depending on whether they are photographs, cartoon type pictures, or animated clips that you sometimes see on web pages. Each type of image is recognized by its file extension. The most common ones are:

Image type	What it is
`.jpg`	The most common photo format. Make sure that your photos are of this type.
`.gif`	The most common format for graphic images, clipart/cartoons, or animated images.
`.png`	Another popular format for images, especially on web sites.
`.bmp`	A high-quality picture file, not really suited for Moodle due to its size. Avoid it.

Time for action-getting a program to help us edit images for Moodle

For this purpose, we need a simple program that will change the size of our photos or other images without losing their quality or distorting them.

If you are using a Mac, you will have a facility known as **Preview**, which does the job we want.

If you have Microsoft Office, there is a very basic image editing program called **Microsoft Picture Manager**, which is worth practicing with.

However, if you are on a PC and don't have Microsoft Office installed in your computer, there is a free program that we're about to use. This program will resize the single photo Liz wants in her label. Furthermore, Liz can show the students all of the photos in the folder at one go. It'scalled **IrfanView**.

1. Go to the web site `http://www.irfanview.com/`.

2. Click on the **IrfanView** download link, as shown in the following screenshot:

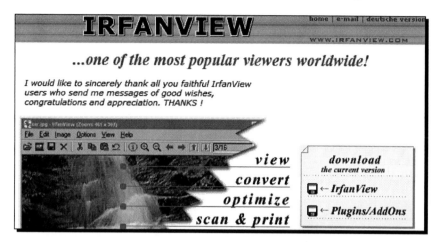

3. Next, click on the button named **Download Now**. If you get a message saying that downloading files is blocked, click on the message and then click on **Download file**.

4. Click on **Run** (if you only have the **Save** option, that's fine too!). If you're prompted to allow this, go ahead and agree. It's perfectly safe!

5. Keep clicking on **Next,** until you get to the following message:

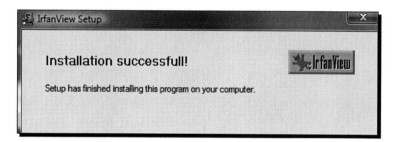

6. Click on **Done**, and you should be taken to IrfanView. If not, click on the icon available at your desktop.

What just happened?

We went to the IrfanView web site and downloaded a free program that will enable us to alter the dimensions of photos and other images that we want to use in Moodle. IrfanView can also edit photos in many other ways. However, we don't have time to investigate all of these. But why not have a look at its other features once you've mastered the resizing?

Time for action-resizing a single photo to display on Moodle

Make sure that you have a reasonably large photo ready. Using IrfanView, let's make the image smaller.

> **1.** Start IrfanView.

> **2.** Select menu option **File | Open**.

> **3.** As with Moodle, navigate to the photo that you want (that ends with the extension .jpg), select it, and click on **Open**.

> **4.** Click on the **Image** tab and then click on **Resize/Resample**. The following screenshot will appear:

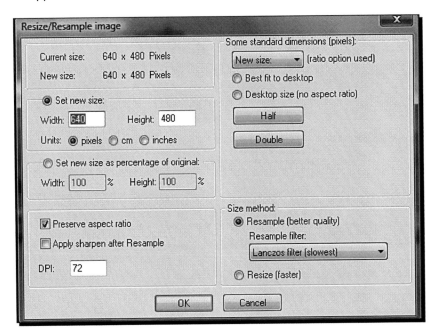

> **5.** If you have an idea about the pixels, you can change the number of **pixels** in the **Width** box. The height will change accordingly, to ensure that the image is not distorted.

6. If you prefer to think in centimeters (**cm**) or **inches**, click on that unit and then change the width.

7. If you wish to make your photo a certain percent smaller than it was before, click on **Set new size as a percentage**, and specify the required percentage.

8. Click on the **OK** button located at the bottom of the window.

9. Select menu option **File | Save as** and (if you want) rename your photo or save over the original.

What just happened?

We used the free program IrfanView to transform a larger image into a smaller image—but, without spoiling its appearance. By selecting the **Preserve aspect ratio** checkbox (as shown in the previous screenshot) we ensured that if we decreased the width, the height would decrease accordingly. You can deselect this checkbox and choose your own width and height ratio, but your photo might look a bit odd. We now have a photo suitably resized for being displayed on Moodle.

Have a go hero-proving the importance of resizing images!

Not convinced? Think it's a lot of effort when you can just upload your photo as it is and change it in Moodle? Well, try a little experiment then.

◆ Upload the largest photo that you have (thousands of pixels, hopefully!) and display it in a Moodle label, resizing it to around 100 x100 pixels.

◆ Then go to IrfanView and resize that same photo properly, to around 100 x100 pixels. Then upload it and display it in a second label.

Notice any differences? If you have a super-fast broadband connection, you might not notice much. However, at the very least, you will find that it takes more time to upload the image first and then resize it, as compared to using IrfanView and then uploading the resized image. Seconds maybe, but as a busy teacher, you can get impatient with every extra moment wasted. If you look closely at the first photo, you will probably see that it looks a bit –well – squashed. The second version is clearer. That's because in the first one, we are singing a three-minute song to a one-minute tune whereas in the second one, the tune and lyrics are both one minute! Finally, and most important of all, if your Internet connection is not that fast, or if any of your students are on dial-up, the first photo will take an age to appear, a bit at a time, whereas the second one, properly resized, will be displayed almost immediately.

Ok, so let's now look at resizing a whole folder of photos, such as Liz's New Orleans ones. It would be a pain to have to go through the above process for every single image; fortunately it isn't necessary with IrfanView.

Time for action-re-sizing several photos, all in one go

Let's learn how to re-size several photos at once.

1. Start IrfanView.

2. Select menu option **File | Batch conversion/Rename**.

3. You will see a screen similar to the following screenshot:

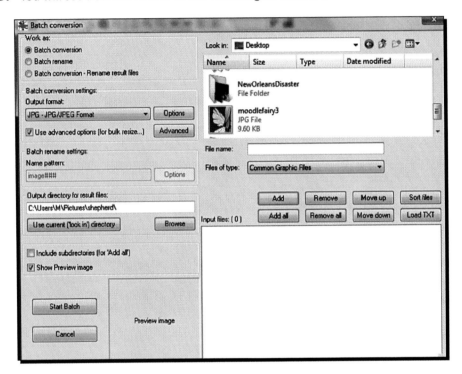

4. Click on **Look in** and navigate to the folder of photos that you want to resize.

5. Click on the folder. The images will appear individually.

6. Click on the **Add all** button. Their file names will appear in the input file box at the bottom of the screen.

7. In the **Output directory**, choose the location to which you want the folder of resized photos to be saved. If you want it in the same place as the current folder, click on **Use current ('look in') directory**.

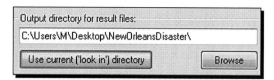

8. Under Batch conversion settings, click on **Advanced**.

9. In the box that is displayed, set your new size, and ignore everything else!

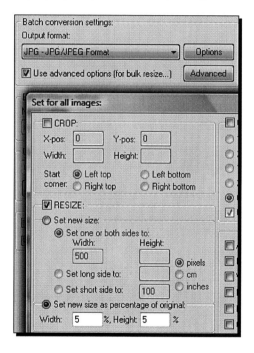

10. Click on **OK**.

11. Back on the main screen, click on **Start Batch**.

12. Sit back and relax as IrfanView does all the work of resizing your photos, for you!

What just happened?

We used IrfanView to resize a whole folder of photos for Moodle. Now when we upload them it will take less time, and they will display better—especially for those of our students whose Internet connection isn't as fast as ours.

There are several ways to have photo slideshows in Moodle. Your Moodle might have its own gallery such as **Lightbox Gallery** or a **Moodle Gallery Module**. If it doesn't, you might consider using an online gallery such as **Flickr**, although you'd have to be careful if you are using images of children. Our colleague Liz is simply going to display them as a directory for the time being.

Showing YouTube videos on Moodle when YouTube is banned

Here's the final practical problem that Liz has presented us with: she's found a couple of really good eye witness amateur videos of the disaster. She's got permission from the owner (**very important**) to use them in her Moodle course, but she can't show them because our school won't allow us to access YouTube! How do we solve that one?

The answer is to wait until we get home and then download the video onto our own computer. Then we can upload it as a regular file into our Moodle course.

There are several ways of downloading YouTube videos. Some of them require you to install something on your own computer, while others ask you for an email address to send you the video. But the one we're going to use here gives us the video pretty much instantaneously.

Time for action-how to download a YouTube video to use on Moodle

Make sure that you have permission to do this! Carefully read YouTube's advice on copyright issues at, `http://help.Youtube.com/support/Youtube/bin/ topic.py?topic=10554`

1. Find your YouTube video and copy (*Ctrl+C*) its web address (URL) as shown in the following screenshot:

2. Go to the web site `http://mediaconverter.org.`

3. Paste (*Ctrl+V*) that video address into the input box, as shown in the following screenshot:

4. Click on **Next step**.

5. Click the drop-down arrow for **---select a file type---** and choose **flv** (You could choose another type, such as **wmv**, but this one will do for us).

6. Click on **Next step** and ignore the next page of instructions.

7. Click on **Next step** again.

8. Sit back and relax while the site does its job!

9. Click on the **DOWNLOAD NOW** link to download the video to somewhere that you can store it ready for Moodle.

What just happened?

We used a free web site service that enabled us to download in five steps a YouTube video that we can now upload to our Moodle course. We found our video's URL on YouTube, entered it on this site and received a link to the file.

You can have your YouTube video emailed to you if you don't mind waiting half an hour or so. Try one of these two sites: `http:// www.zamzar.com` or `http://www.youconvertit.com`. You can also download a program that will download your video and convert it to a different type of file, if you want, via web site `http://Youtubedownload.altervista.org/`

Did you notice when going through that process that many different video (and audio) file types were on offer? As we've looked at document file extensions and image file extensions, now might be a good time to cast a glance at the type of multimedia file Moodle prefers. Here's a simple table explaining the most common formats. There are others, but these are the ones that we're most likely to want to use.

File extension	Sound/video?	How useful is it for us in Moodle?
`.flv`	video	A flash video file such as those you get on YouTube. Plays well if you have multimedia filters enabled.
`.wmv`	video	The kind of file we made with Windows Movie Maker.
`.avi`	video	A large video file type. Moodle will play it, but it's too big, really!
`.mpg`	video	Tends to be quite small in size.
`.mov`	video	A **Quicktime** videos can be quite large. Check their size!
`.mp3`	sound	The best sound file format for Moodle. We set up Audacity for these.
`.wav`	sound	A Windows sound file. These can be large and won't play in the player.

If you have large video files, you might want to convert them to the `.flv` format using one of the web sites mentioned above. They will load up more quickly and play better in Moodle. And as this chapter is all about making Moodle work, that's a good idea.

Have a go hero-display a YouTube video in Moodle

Simple! We've done this several times before! We haven't used a `.flv` file, but the process is the same. Check whether your Moodle Admin has the `.flv` filter enabled in site administration.

- Use select menu option **Add a Resource | Compose a web page**
- Select **Blank text**, and then click on the **Hyperlink** (chain) icon
- Link to the `.flv` file, which you have uploaded or will upload now, and then save the changes
- Admire your work!

Summary

In this chapter, we've focused on making sure that everything on our course page displays properly for our students. We've also helped a new Moodler ensure that her teaching materials are easily accessible. We have:

- Provided a link on our course page to OpenOffice—a free alternative to MS Office—for students such as Joe, who don't have Microsoft Office Word at home
- Used OpenOffice's pdf conversion facility to change documents into a format that anyone can easily read
- Downloaded and used iSpring, a free program that converts slideshows to a format that all children can view without difficulty
- Downloaded an image resizing and editing program, IrfanView, to help colleague Liz display her photos better on Moodle
- Learned how to allow YouTube videos on Moodle, even though the site is not allowed in our school.

We can be happy in the knowledge that even though Joe's Internet connection is slow, and he doesn't have MS Office, he'll still be able to view his teacher's resources. And he'll have no excuse not to have done his homework!

9

Advanced tips and tricks

This chapter gives a taste of Moodle level two! It looks at how we can use the more advanced features of Moodle, plus some optional features, to enhance our teaching further. The previous chapters contained everything that you need to build and run a fully interactive Moodle course. However, once you're familiar with those resources and activities, you might want to read the following pages to stretch your skills a little more.

In this chapter, we're going to complete our course by:

- ◆ Challenging our students' newly acquired knowledge through a decision making exercise
- ◆ Ensuring their learning continues, even after the end of the unit, by giving them links to the latest rivers and flooding news

We're going to find out how we can use Moodle's optional extras to:

- ◆ Get the students to complete the evaluation of an entire course, to help us review it for the next year
- ◆ Present the students with a certificate of success

And finally, we're going to:

- ◆ Revamp our course homepage to make it look more like a traditional web page— believing in the phrase, **Appearance is Everything**!

Using Moodle to get our students to make decisions

Have you ever done any of those fun online quizzes that abound, such as 'How attractive are you?', 'Which famous person do you most resemble?' and so on. They start by asking you questions such as 'Are you male or female?' and then tailor their answers to suit your selection. These activities work by having alternative **branches** depending on what we choose each time we click one of the buttons. If you are good at slideshow presentations, you can do similar kinds of things by hyperlinking an action button to a particular slide. Moodle has this **branching** feature too, in the **Lesson** module. We're going to use it now to create a decision making exercise for our students. It's great for those higher level thinking skills that we're meant to encourage in the students. We are going to ask our class to put themselves in the shoes of a nine year old girl, Milly, who is about to experience a major flood in her road. They have to make choices for her and her family according to what they have learned about the dangers of flooding. What they choose will have an effect on Milly's safety—and their score!

A Moodle Lesson is not what we think of as a lesson, in the literal sense! It is a series of connected pages that you'll use to direct the students through a certain course of action. It can be used for DMEs, for step-by-step independent learning, or for other activities requiring linking sections. It is very complex to set up. We are only touching its surface out here.

Time for action-creating a decision-making exercise (DME)

Let's create a decision making exercise, which will test the decision making skills and spontaneity of the students.

1. With editing turned on, in the topic section you want, click on **Add an activity** and then click on **Lesson**.

2. In the **Name** box, give a title to your exercise, on which your students will click on to start the exercise.

3. For our basic activity, set the **Maximum number of answers/branches** to **2** and the **Maximum grade** to **10**, as shown in the following screenshot. Use other numbers when you try it out yourself, some other time!

4. From the **Display ongoing score** drop-down menu, select **Yes**.

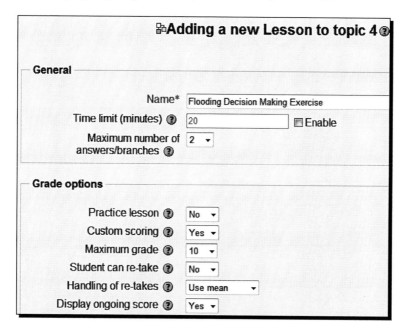

5. Ignore everything else! This is just a taster, remember.

6. Click on **Save and Display**. You'll get the screen, as shown in the following screenshot:

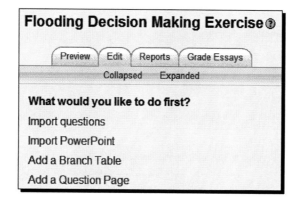

7. Click on the **Add a Branch Table** link.

8. Enter a scene-setting introduction in the **Page contents:** box, as shown in the following screenshot:

9. Scroll down and click on the **Add Branch Table** link.

10. In the **Actions** block on the next screen, click on the **Add a page...** drop-down menu and select the **Question** option.

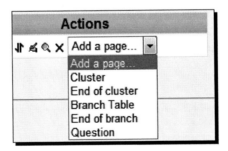

11. Click on the **Multiple Choice** tab at the top of the screen.

12. In the **Page title:** box, enter a question.

13. In the **Page contents:** box, specify the first decision to be made, as shown in the following screenshot:

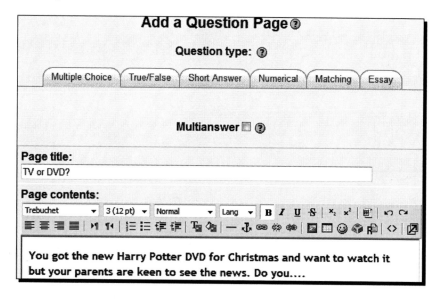

14. In the **Answer 1** box and the **Response 1** box, enter the **correct** answer and your feedback for it, respectively.

15. In the **Answer 2** box and the **Response 2** box, enter the **incorrect** answer and your feedback for it, respectively..

16. Set **Score 1** to **0** and **Score 2** to **1**.

17. Set **Jump 1** and the **Jump 2** to **Next page**.

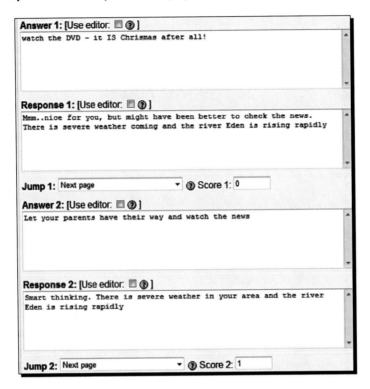

18. Scroll down and click on the **Add a Question Page** link.

19. In the **Actions** block on the next screen, click on the **Add a page...** drop-down menu next to your last page (in our case, **TV or DVD?**) and select **Question**.

20. Click on the **Multiple Choice** tab at the top of the screen.

21. In the **Page title:** block, enter a short question.

22. In the **Page Contents** block, set out the decision to be made, as shown in the following screenshot:

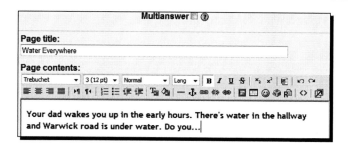

23. In the **Answer 1** box and the **Response 1** box, enter the **correct** answer and your feedback for it, respectively.

24. In the **Answer 2** box and the **Response 2** box, enter the **incorrect** answer and your feedback for it, respectively.

25. Set **Score 1** to **0** and **Score 2** to **1**.

26. Set both **Jump 1** and **Jump 2** to **Next page**.

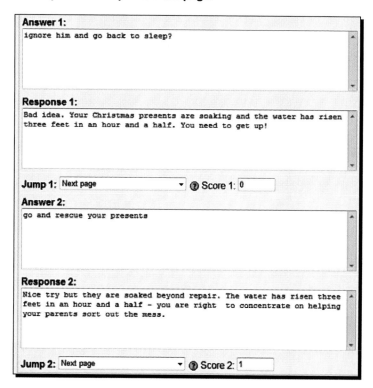

27. Scroll down and click on the **Add a Question Page** link.

What just happened?

Phew! Let's just take a break for a moment.

We used the **Lesson** module to set up a decision making exercise. We asked our students to put themselves in the place of a girl in the North of England whose house was flooded out a few years back. This role play is based on a true story and thus, at the end of my lesson I actually linked the story on the BBC News web site to our Moodle course so that my students could see that their decision making had been done for real.

We used a Branch Table to set the scene, then linked it to a multi-choice question page where we gave the students two options, depending on which they are given some appropriate feedback from us, and a score of either 0 or 1. We linked both choices to another question and repeated the process.

So far, we have had two choices and two points. We need to carry on until we feel that enough action has been taken. Our DME exercise is given a score out of 10.

Have a go hero-carry on decision making!

When we clicked on the **Add a Question Page** link, we got to a screen similar to the one shown in the following screenshot:

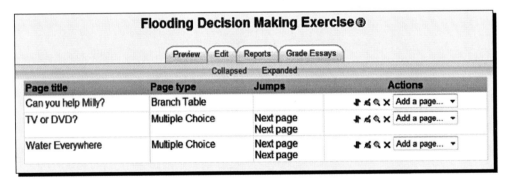

- In the **Actions** block, click on **Add a Page** next to your last page (in our case, **Water Everywhere**) and select **Question** from the drop-down list.
- Choose **Multiple Choice** from the tabs available at the top.
- Add another decision with its answers, responses, and scores.
- Keep going!
- Why not make a couple of scores more than 1?

Time for action-finishing and viewing our DME

Once we're satisfied with the activity, it's time for a final page—rounding it all off.
Here's how:

1. In the **Actions** block, link your last question page to **Branch Table**.

2. Prepare the summary of comments, as shown here:

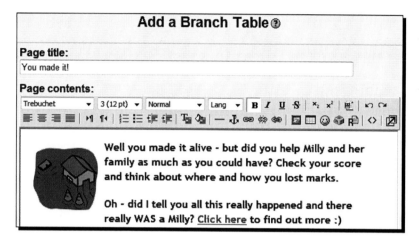

3. In the **Description 1:** block, provide a goodbye comment.

4. In the **Jump 1** block, choose **End of lesson**.

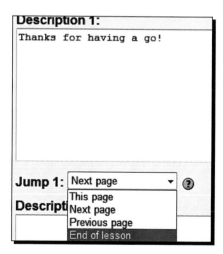

5. On the next screen, click the **Preview** tab to test that all of the connected pages work. Try the alternative answers—does it all follow on appropriately?

6. Go to your course page, switch to **Student View** and check whether the scores work the way they should.

7. If it all works correctly pat yourself on the back for having made a start in one of Moodle's more advanced activities!

Keeping our students up-to-date with the latest news

Apart from adding more strings to our teaching bow, the aim of this chapter is to give you an insight into some of the more complex features in Moodle. We just used a **Lesson,** which was an activity module. We're now going to work on a Moodle block. This particular block would have been too much to take in at the start of the book. However, with a few hours of practice under our belts, we can do this one. No worries!

You might see that some web sites have links to news items that change constantly when new events happen. You can actually choose to have these news items come straight into your computer or your email, if you wish. Some people do this to get specific news of their interest, for example, sports news or education news. We're going to get the latest geographical events and put them straight into our Moodle course by using something called **RSS (Really Simple Syndication).**

RSS is simply a type of web page that sends out news updates and/or details. Moodle's RSS block is a function that lets us add links from various news sources so that as soon as any big event occurs we are alerted about it on our Moodle.

Of course, we need to find some news sources first, and there's a wide choice out there. Many news or information web sites have an RSS feed, and you can find this on their home page, next to an icon that looks like the following image:

As our pupils are focusing on rivers and flooding, let's go and find a couple of relevant RSS feeds for Moodle. We'll get the latest updates for the river Thames in London, plus some world weather news.

Time for action-getting some appropriate news feeds for our topic

We know that RSS feeds are used to publish the latest updates and news. Let's find a news source that supports RSS feeds and gives out information on river Thames, and add this source into our Moodle course.

1. Go to the web site `http://riverconditions.visitthames.co.uk/`.

2. Scroll down to the RSS logo on the right and click the words **Click here to subscribe via RSS**.

3. Copy (using the *Ctrl+C* keys on the keyboard) the URL (web site address) that appears next, which will be `http://riverconditions.visitthames.co.uk/feed.rss`.

4. Paste (using the *Ctrl+V* keys on the keyboard) this URL into Notepad or a Word document, to keep it safe for later use.

5. Go to the BBC weather feeds web site on `http://tinyurl.com/2ya9hu`.

6. Click on **International Weather Headlines**, located at the rightmost side of the screen.

7. Copy the URL that appears next, which will be `http://feeds.bbc.co.uk/weather/feeds/rss/headlines/intl_weather_headline.xml`.

8. Paste this second URL into Notepad or a Word document, to keep safe for later use.

What just happened?

We got a couple of RSS feed links that we can add to our Moodle RSS block. We found them by looking for the words RSS or the RSS logo on the sites that we are interested in. If we put the two URLs that we have copied into our Notepad or Word document into our Moodle course page, we will be informed as soon as there are any flood alerts in London, or whenever there are serious weather conditions around the world.

So how do we get these feeds and others like them into Moodle? By making the most of our newly-found advanced skills and setting up the RSS block!

 To use the RSS feeds in Moodle, you need to ensure that they are enabled by your Administrator. Also, you need to ensure that the Administrator has given you, as a teacher, the permission to define new RSS feeds on the site.

Time for action-keeping our students informed with a Moodle RSS block

We have searched for the news sources that provide us with essential weather updates. We have also copied the URL of an RSS feed for a weather news web sites. It's now time to add these RSS feeds into our Moodle course.

1. With editing turned on, go to **Blocks**, click on **Add,** and select **Remote RSS feeds.**

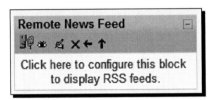

2. Click on the **Click here to configure this block to display RSS feeds** link, in the **Remote News Feed** block.

3. In the screen that is displayed next, click on the **Manage all my feeds** tab.

4. In the **Add a news feed URL** box, paste (using the *Ctrl+V* keys on the keyboard) the URL (web site address) of one of the feeds (or one of your own) that we have saved in the Notepad or the Word document.

5. In the **Custom title** field, give the RSS feed a name that the students will understand. Now, our window appears as shown in the following screenshot:

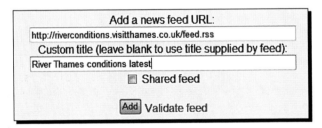

6. Click on the **Validate Feed** link. This just checks that the newly-added RSS feed is working.

7. Next, click on the **Add** button.

8. When the next screen appears, follow the same procedure for the other feed (or feeds that you might have).

9. Click on the **Configure this block** tab at the top of the window.

10. Select the checkboxes for the feeds that you want to include.

11. Next to the **Title**, specify a name for your block that will be seen in Moodle.

12. Click on **Save changes**.

What just happened?

We just added a block that enables us to show the latest news from some weather web sites, which we chose to allow into Moodle. We pasted the URLs of the RSS feed pages into the block. These feeds will now be displayed on our course page, with changing information depending on the occurrence of the news events. If we go to **Student View**, we will be able to see how the newly-added block will be displayed to our pupils. Ours is shown in the following screenshot:

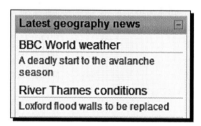

The students just need to click on the descriptions under the headings, and they'll be taken to the site that gives them the latest news. So the students can be on the ball during and after our Rivers and Flooding topic!

Finishing off—what else can Moodle do for me?

In learning how to create a DME with a **Lesson** and how to add the latest news with an **RSS block**, we looked at two slightly more advanced features of Moodle. There are many more features that Moodle has to offer to enhance our teaching, but not all of them are available on the standard Moodle web site that most schools have installed. However, if you have a sympathetic Moodle Administrator who has complete control of your Moodle installation, it is very easy to **plug-in** extra options that can be very useful and also a lot of fun. One Moodler has compared Moodle to a Lego set. You start with the basic building bricks and then, as you become more experienced, you can add different types of bricks to fulfill different functions.

The next section will teach you what you can do with some of the extra plug-ins available on the main Moodle site, `http://www.moodle.org`. The following table suggests a handful of plug-ins that I've found work well with children in the age group of 7-14. You might like to ask your Administrator sweetly (or maybe bribe them with chocolate!) if they could add one or two of these to your school's Moodle course page. Let's just have a brief look at a couple of these plug-ins and learn how they could make a fitting conclusion to our course.

Optional plug-in name	What it is	How we could use it
Questionnaire	A customizable survey module (ignore the standard **survey** option in Moodle).	For evaluations by students or teachers. We could use it to improve our course.
Feedback	A simpler version of the questionnaire.	For quick evaluations.
Certificate	Generates a personalized certificate.	Great for the end of our course!
Lightbox gallery	An easy image gallery that displays folders of photos in a flashy kind of way	Useful for people like our colleague Liz who want a simple way to display photos.
Game module	Takes words from the Glossary or Quiz and puts them into eight different types of games.	We can't have too many games that work with Moodle's grade book.
Stamp collection	Gives students reward stamps.	A great motivator, just like a gold stars in the students' books.
Book	Linked pages, a bit like a mini web site	Handy for showcasing students' work.

Evaluating our course with a Moodle questionnaire

It is important for our own professional development that we constantly strive to improve our teaching, and adapt it according to our successes and setbacks. For this, we need the input of our students (it's the **Student Voice** concept, for which Moodle is perfectly suited). We could use Moodle's **Choice** activity module as a very basic survey. But the issue with this is that the pupils are able to respond to only single word, or short phrase suggestions that we give them. If we want a more detailed evaluation of our efforts in Moodle, the optional **Questionnaire** module fits the bill perfectly, as we can include choice-type option button answers and also give them free rein to comment in the text boxes. And don't think that just because the students haven't reached double figures, they aren't capable of giving insightful opinions!

There seems little point in going step-by-step through the operation of a Questionnaire if your Moodle doesn't have it. However, I thought it would be useful to have a glimpse of one, just to give you more reasons to request it from your admin! You won't have any problems setting this up, or any other optional modules.

Now, you have learned the basics of Moodle and have gone through a few more complex aspects, earlier on in this chapter. The following screenshot shows the first few questions of our Rivers and Flooding Review:

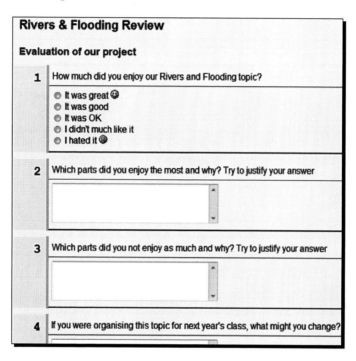

All of the results are saved and collated, and you can even download them as a spreadsheet if you like that sort of thing.

Rewarding our students efforts with a certificate

Who doesn't like getting a certificate? All students, and usually boys who play it cool and pretend not to be bothered, actually feel proud to be recognized for their achievements. So having Moodle produce a personalized certificate will give them a real buzz, whether they admit it or not. Why not try to get the optional certificate module for your Moodle? You decide the criteria for students obtaining the certificate, and you can customize its appearance. Once the student has been awarded the completion certificate, the student clicks on a link in the course home page to receive his/her certificate as a pdf file—which they can save or print. Do you remember Joe from Chapter 8, who claimed that he couldn't work on Moodle as he didn't have MS Word? Even he made it to the end, and here's his certificate to prove it:

A nice touch, isn't it? The certificate can be made even more attractive if you spend some time on it. You can alter the color and border, add grades, a signature, a logo, and so on. This brings us to our final section. It's all about looking good.

Making our course home page look more like a web page

As we approach the end of the book, let's just take a look back at Chapter 1. There, I pointed out that, for the young students we are teaching, appearance is everything. It was important for us to make our course page appealing to the eye, and so we spent some time in adding images, changing font styles and colors, and trying to keep our resources in a neat order. We have a busy course, full of content, now. Although our Moodle course has got lots to keep our youngsters occupied, it still has that rather conventional Moodle layout of different topic sections, where we have to scroll down to reach the activity that we want.

On ordinary web sites, the pages are much shorter, and you can get to the other sections by clicking on the text or on image hyperlinks. Now that it's complete, how about making our course look like a normal web page instead of a Moodle course page? Let's be radical; let's redo the whole thing! Instead of having four sections with activities that stretch far down the page, let's just keep the page short, with an image for each unit. We could then click on the relevant image to take us to that unit's activities. We can have something similar to what is shown in the following screenshot.

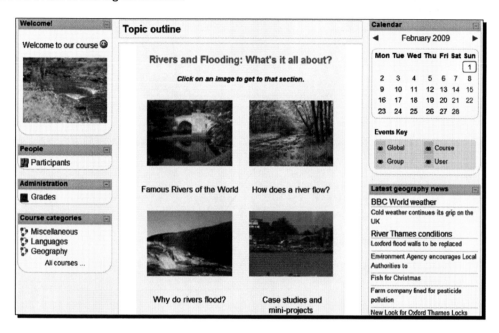

Our students can see everything in one window—no need to scroll down! But where are all the activities? And how is it done? We can't hide them from the eye because then they are not accessible to students at all. Thus, we need to find some other cunning way of hiding them, but still making them available. But first, we need to set that top section up with the image links.

Have a go hero-source and resize suitable images for each topic section

The plan is to replace each numbered topic section with an image, which will hyperlink to the activities in that section. Your first mission, then, is to find some suitable images, such as .jpg photos or .gif clipart of your choice. Then, you have to make them all the same size, so that they look correct on the page. Mine are 160 X 120 pixels; that's not a bad size. 100 X 100 pixels might even be better if you want your image to be square in shape.

Got them? Now let's upload them into the course and let's get started!

Time for action-adding image links to our topic sections

Let's learn how to add images into our Moodle course, which when clicked will take you to a new web site.

1. With editing turned on, click on the editing icon for **Topic 0**.

2. In the toolbar, click on the **Insert Table** icon, located to the left of the smiley.

3. If you're copying my layout, choose **2** columns and **4** rows. Choose **0** for border, cell spacing, and padding.

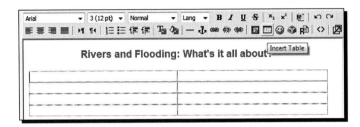

4. Click on the **Full Screen Editor** icon located at the bottom of the screen, on the far right.

5. Click in the upper-left cell.

6. Click on the image icon and insert your first topic image. Centre by using with the HTML editor centering icon.

7. In the cell directly below the image icon, add the topic name and centre it.

8. Repeat this with the other three images and topic titles, as shown in the following screenshot:

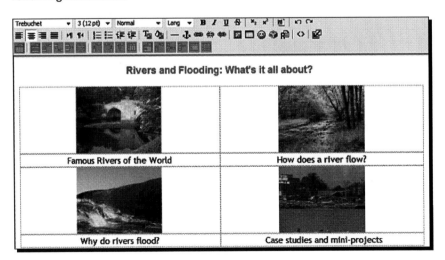

9. Click the **Full Screen Editor** icon again to close it and save changes.

What just happened?

We went into the editing area of **Topic 0** and created a table, into which we added images that will link to our different units of work. We put the names of the units underneath, to help with identification. Eventually, this table in **Topic 0** will be all that the students will see, and they will click on the images (or the text if you prefer) to access their work.

So now, we need to create some web pages to add our activities into. Then, we can link those pages to the relevant image in **Topic 0**. Let's start with **Topic 1**—Famous Rivers of the World.

Time for action-putting our activities into web pages

There are various ways to go about this, but the following way is the one that I prefer:

1. Open up a Word document, Notepad or a similar text editing program into which you can paste some URLs.

2. Go to **Topic 1**, and right-click on the first resource or activity.

3. Click on **Properties**.

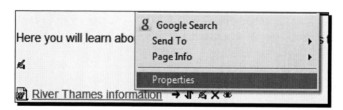

4. Copy (*Ctrl+C*) the Address or the URL that will appear, and then paste it (*Ctrl+V*) into your text document.

5. In your text document, type a name to remind you which resource or activity the link was for.

6. Repeat this process with all of the resources and activities in topic 1.

7. Keep your text document safe, and scroll down to the bottom of the final topic.

8. Under **Add a resource**, choose **Compose a web page**.

9. Type in an introduction to the topic and paste in the resources and activities hyperlinks from your text document, making sure that they open in a new window.

10. Save it and display it. It will look something like this:

Rivers and Flooding

Moodle ▶ R & F ▶ Resources ▶ **Topic 1**

In this topic we're going to investigate some famous rivers of the world. You'll learn about the longest, deepest, widest rivers throughout the globe ☺

Here is some information about rivers in the UK. If you can't get them to come up on your computer, you can download a program that will help you by clicking here

1. Click here to read about the **Thames**
2. Click here to read about the **Severn**
3. Click here for an information sheet about **Rivers in Wales**
4. Click here for an information sheet about **Rivers in Scotland**

Next up we're going around the World in Rivers...

Remember that because this is a web page, we have the freedom to make it attractive, with images, hyperlinks, and so on. **Topic 1** looks pretty basic as it's just an introduction, with some word-processed documents. Just imagine how much fun we can have setting up the web page for our interactive, multimedia, Web 2.0 case studies in **Topic 4**!

What just happened?

Basically, we went to **Topic 1**, copied the links to the resources and activities by right-clicking and then clicking on **Properties** in order to get the URL, and then pasted them into a Moodle web page, which we embellished with some friendly words and colorful images. The idea is that our students will click on the **Topic 1** image in **Topic 0** page, and this will take them directly to the **Topic 1** web page. They can then select, from this web page, the activity that they need to do next.

Thus, we need to go back to that table of images in **Topic 0** and then link the web page that we just developed to the first image. But that's easy for an advanced Moodler.

Time for action-link the topic web page to its image

Just use the same principles as before. There's nothing new to learn here.

1. Right-click on the web page and copy its URL.

2. Click the editing icon for **Topic 0** and click on the first image, which is for **Topic 1**.

3. Click on the **Hyperlink** icon and paste the URL of the web page into the hyperlink box.

4. Save, and check whether it works!

The same process we went through for **Topic 1** now needs to be repeated for the other three topics. Are you up for it?

Have a go hero-link the other topics to their images

It's just a question of taking a topic section, copying its resource links onto a new Moodle web page, prettying up the web page, and then linking it to its matching image up at the top of our course. Once you have done that with all of the other sections, there is only one more job left to do, which is, to get the effect that we saw earlier.

Concealing our activities to make our course page neater

This is the crafty part! The secret is in hiding the topics within the activities—without closing the student's eyes or making the content unavailable. However, we do need to have one topic in view, because Moodle (quite rightly) won't let us have a course with zero topics. Therefore, we'll have **Topic 1** as empty and then cunningly conceal the four topic sections that have all of our stuff added to them (including those web pages that we just made and added at the bottom of our final topic).

Time for action-making our course page look more like a web page

Let's learn how to make our Moodle course page look prettier, and more like a web page.

1. In the **Administration** block, click on **Settings**.

2. Change the number of topics to one more than you already have (in our case, five).

3. Save the changes.

4. Go back to the central section and use the up arrow, to move the blank new topic into the position for **Topic 1**.

5. Go back to the **Administration** block and click on **Settings** again.

6. Change the number of topics to one.

7. Save your changes.

8. Done! Forget the coffee! Crack open the champagne!

What just happened?

We performed a massive con trick! We made a course with five sections, we made the first section empty and set the next four full of good content. We got Moodle to display only the first one and keep the others out of sight. But just because we set the course to display only one topic, it doesn't mean that the others are gone forever. Our efforts over nine chapters can't be deleted that easily. They're just hiding, and waiting to be made available for use, but actually not on the page. If we ever want to reveal them again some other time, it's a simple case of adjusting the settings in the **Administration** block.

Summary

In this chapter, we've risen to the challenge of advanced Moodling, using our recently-acquired skills to tackle more complex features. We have:

- Created a **Decision Making Exercise (DME)** using a Moodle **Lesson**
- Provided our class with the latest news by using a **Remote RSS block**
- Gained an insight into some optional extras of Moodle, such as a **Questionnaire** and a **Certificate**
- Added a finishing touch to our course by making it look more like a web page

We've learned that Moodle offers a wide variety of ways for our students to learn—from us, from each other, and also on their own. We've learned that working on Moodle isn't just about uploading word-processed worksheets (which might not even be viewable to some of our youngsters). Rather, it's about providing opportunities to engage, to explore, and above all to enjoy the pleasures of acquiring and evaluating new knowledge in a modern, multi-media environment.

I hope that you have as much fun using Moodle with your classes as I do. If you need any more help, come along to the forums on `http://www.moodle.org`, where there are over half a million enthusiasts, myself included, who will be keen to provide you with assistance.

Happy Moodling!

Index

face icons 10
factsheet, displaying 29
Google Map, displaying 150, 151
HTML editor, using 15
image, adding to HTML block 20, 21
image links, adding to topics 206, 207
images, uploading 18-20
issues, embedding maps 152
look, modifying 39-41
middle section, customizing 14
modifying 9, 209
modifying, like web page 204, 205
new block, adding 10
side blocks, creating 13
standard blocks 11, 12
story telling, with Go Animate site 157
topic web page, linking to image 208, 209
courses block 11

D

database
    add entry tab 56
    add tab 55
    create a new field option 54
    field description block 55
    field name block 55
    height 55
    introduction block 54
    name block 54
    Save and Display option 54
    setting up 54-56
    width 55
decision-making exercise
    about 190
    Actions block 192
    Add a Branch Table 191
    creating 190-196
    Display ongoing score drop-down menu 191
    finishing 197
    Maximum grade 190
    Multiple Choice tab 193
    Name box 190
    Page contents: box 193
    Page title: box 193
    Question option 192
    viewing 198

discussion forum. *See* **forum**
display mode, choice 58
DME. *See* **decision-making exercise**

E

each person posts 1 discussion, forum 47

F

feedback plug-in 202
fields 54
fling the teacher game
    creating 117-119
    finding 115
    playing 122
    setting up 116, 117
    uploading, on Moodle 119-122
forum
    each person posts 1 discussion forum 47
    force everyone to be subscribed option 46
    forum introduction option 46
    forum name option 45
    forum type option 45
    maximum attachment size option 46
    moderating 47
    need for 48
    post threshold for blocking option 46
    Q and A forum 47
    read tracking option 46
    setting up 45, 46
    single simple discussion forum 47
    standard forum 47
    using, need for 48

G

game
    alien abduction (hangman) game 102
    bin game 105
    bish bash bosh game 107
    fling the teacher game 115
    WordWeb game from Spellmaster 112
game module plug-in 202
global search block 11
glossary
    add a new entry 53
    allow comments box 52

approved by default field 52
concept field 53
creating 51-53
description block 51
description field 53
name option 51
Google Map
  displaying, on course page 150, 151
  embedding, on Moodle 150, 151
  embedding, issues 152
groups, wiki 69

H

hot potatoes
  about 72
  downloading 72-74
  finding 72
  JCloze 74
  JCross 74
  JMatach 74
  JMix 74
  JQuiz 74
  match activity, creating 77, 78
  match activity, uploading on Moodle 80
  pictures, adding 90, 91
  rivers matching to continents exercise, JMatch
    hot potatoes used 74-76
  rivers matching to continents exercise, upload-
    ing on Moodle 77
  self-marking crossword exercise creating, JCross
    hot potatoes used 83-86
  self-marking crossword exercise creating, JMix
    hot potatoes used 86-88
  self-marking gap-fill exercise creating, JCloze hot
    potatoes used 82
  self-marking multiple-choice quiz creating,
    JQuiz hot potatoes used 88, 89
  The masher 74
  words matching with pictures exercise creating,
    JMatch hot potatoes used 90, 91
  words matching with pictures exercise,
    uploading on Moodle 92
  warnings 92
HTML 14
HTML block 11
  about 14

configuring 13
image, adding 20, 21
hyperlink, creating to other web site 33

I

icons
  1, indents to the right 41
  2, moves up or down 41
  3, text editing 41
  4, delete 41
  5, item hiding 41
  about 40
images
  .bmp, image 178
  .gif, image 178
  .jpg, image 178
  .png, image 178
  editing, IrfanView downloading 178, 179
  editing, IrfanView used 178, 179
  resizing, importance 181
  several images, resizing 182-184
  single image resizing, IrfanView used 180, 181
  types 178
IrfanView
  downloading 179
  several images, resizing 182-184
  single image, resizing 180, 181
  used, for image editing 178, 179
iSpring
  used, PowerPoint slideshows converting to flash
    files 174, 176

J

JCloze hot potatoes
  about 74
  self-marking gap-fill exercise, creating 82
JCross hot potatoes
  about 74
  self-marking crossword exercise, creating 83,
    85, 86
JMatch formats
  drag/drop 77
  flash card 77
  standard 77
JMatch hot potatoes
  appearance tab 76

Packt Open Source Project Royalties

When we sell a book written on an Open Source project, we pay a royalty directly to that project. Therefore by purchasing Moodle for Teaching 7-14 Year Olds, Packt will have given some of the money received to the Moodle Project.

In the long term, we see ourselves and you—customers and readers of our books—as part of the Open Source ecosystem, providing sustainable revenue for the projects we publish on. Our aim at Packt is to establish publishing royalties as an essential part of the service and support a business model that sustains Open Source.

If you're working with an Open Source project that you would like us to publish on, and subsequently pay royalties to, please get in touch with us.

Writing for Packt

We welcome all inquiries from people who are interested in authoring. Book proposals should be sent to authors@packtpub.com. If your book idea is still at an early stage and you would like to discuss it first before writing a formal book proposal, contact us; one of our commissioning editors will get in touch with you.

We're not just looking for published authors; if you have strong technical skills but no writing experience, our experienced editors can help you develop a writing career, or simply get some additional reward for your expertise.

About Packt Publishing

Packt, pronounced 'packed', published its first book "Mastering phpMyAdmin for Effective MySQL Management" in April 2004 and subsequently continued to specialize in publishing highly focused books on specific technologies and solutions.

Our books and publications share the experiences of your fellow IT professionals in adapting and customizing today's systems, applications, and frameworks. Our solution-based books give you the knowledge and power to customize the software and technologies you're using to get the job done. Packt books are more specific and less general than the IT books you have seen in the past. Our unique business model allows us to bring you more focused information, giving you more of what you need to know, and less of what you don't.

Packt is a modern, yet unique publishing company, which focuses on producing quality, cutting-edge books for communities of developers, administrators, and newbies alike. For more information, please visit our website: www.PacktPub.com.

Moodle 1.9 E-Learning Course Development

ISBN: 978-1-847193-53-7   Paperback: 360 pages

A complete guide to successful learning using Moodle

1. Updated for Moodle version 1.9

2. Straightforward coverage of installing and using the Moodle system

3. Working with Moodle features in all learning environments

4. A unique course-based approach focuses your attention on designing well-structured, interactive, and successful courses

Moodle Teaching Techniques

ISBN: 978-1-847192-84-4   Paperback: 200 pages

Creative Ways to Use Moodle for Constructing Online Learning Solutions

1. Applying your teaching techniques through Moodle

2. Creative uses for Moodle's standard features

3. Workarounds, providing alternative solutions

4. **Abundantly illustrated with screenshots of the solutions you'll build**

5. Especially good for university and professional teachers

Please check **www.PacktPub.com** for information on our titles

Moodle Course Conversion: Beginner's Guide

ISBN: 978-1-847195-24-1   Paperback: 294 pages

Taking existing classes online quickly with the Moodle LMS

1. No need to start from scratch! This book shows you the quickest way to start using Moodle and e-learning, by bringing your existing lesson materials into Moodle.

2. Move your existing course notes, worksheets, and resources into Moodle quickly then improve your course, taking advantage of multimedia and collaboration.

3. Moving marking online – no more backbreaking boxes of assignments to lug to and from school or college

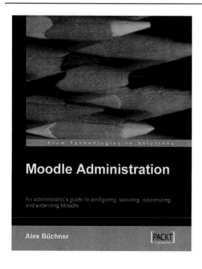

Moodle Administration

ISBN: 978-1-847195-62-3   Paperback: 357 pages

An administrator's guide to configuring, securing, customizing, and extending Moodle

1. A complete guide for planning, installing, optimizing, customizing, and configuring Moodle

2. Secure, back up, and restore your VLE

3. Extending and networking Moodle

Please check **www.PacktPub.com** for information on our titles

3393999

Made in the USA